HIDING *from the* NAZIS

TALES *of* ATROCITY *and* RESISTANCE:
First-Person Stories of Teens in the Holocaust

HIDING *from the* NAZIS

Hallie Murray and Linda Jacobs Altman

Enslow Publishing
101 W. 23rd Street
Suite 240
New York, NY 10011
USA
enslow.com

Introduction

Adolf Hitler became popular in Germany through a combination of charisma and a nationalist agenda. Germany had recently suffered a significant loss in World War I, and many Germans were incredibly angry and scared after Germany's defeat at the hands of the Allied forces and the subsequent collapse of the German economy. They were looking for a leader who would improve the economy and provide a scapegoat for all of their anger and fear. Hitler offered both: he promised to help Germany rise from its economic depression, and he and his party, the Nazis, spread the idea that all of Germany's problems could be blamed on people who lived in Germany but were not, according to Hitler, actually German: the Jews.

After being appointed chancellor in 1933, Hitler began to transform Germany into his idea of a "racial state." He based it on the notion that the Germanic and Nordic peoples, whom he called Aryans, were a master race, superior to all other peoples. His racial state would institutionalize or destroy deformed or otherwise defective people. It would sterilize people with genetic defects so they could not have children. It would reduce the population of Russians, Poles, and other ethnic groups that Hitler classed as "subhuman" and use the survivors as slaves.

Adolf Hitler was known as a charismatic and compelling speaker who stoked hate and encouraged violence in his followers. He became the leader of the Nazi Party in 1921 and chancellor of Germany in 1933.

Most of all, it would "cleanse" this society of Jews. Hitler hated Jews above all other people. He regarded them as dangerous parasites who corrupted anything they touched. Many have tried to explain this irrational hatred, but no one has fully succeeded. Whatever the reason, Hitler's anti-Semitism, or hatred of Jews, went deep. On many occasions, he spoke plainly about his plans for the Jews, especially with his staff:

> From the rostrum of the Reichstag [German parliament] I prophesied to Jewry [that], in the event of [war], the Jew would disappear from Europe. That race of criminals has on its conscience the two million dead of the first World War, and now already hundreds of thousands more. Let nobody tell me that . . . we can't park them in the marshy parts of Russia! . . . It's not a bad idea, by the way, that public rumour [says we have] a plan to exterminate the Jews. Terror is a [beneficial] thing.[1]

According to Hitler, all of Germany's problems, especially those that had been caused by their losses during World War I, could be blamed on Jews. In order to improve Germany, he believed, as did the Nazis and many regular Germans who were convinced by Nazi ideologies, that all of the Jews needed to be somehow eliminated from German society. At first, it seemed like this elimination would come in the form of segregation and persecution, but eventually it became clear that Jews and other populations faced torture and death if they were unable to escape in time.

Many people were indeed able to escape Nazi-occupied territory before things became too dire, but others were forced to go into hiding: some just until they, too, could escape to a better life elsewhere, some for the duration of World War II, and some until they were found and brutally murdered or sent to concentration camps. Nazi Germany was a terrifying place for everyone who did not fit into the stereotype of the Aryan, and people hid in a wide range of places, including in secret bunkers, hidden rooms, and even in plain sight.

Chapter 1

To Leave or to Stay?

Although Hitler's intentions seem clear in retrospect, he was not so forthcoming about his plans to the public, though many of his followers were. Hitler was the leader of the Nazi party, and after being appointed chancellor in 1933 he began to take steps toward making the Nazi party the only political party in Germany. In 1934, when the German president died, Hitler became the sole leader of Germany, and the nation became a totalitarian state where it was illegal not to be a Nazi. The party became even more powerful and continued to create laws that slowly stripped Jews and other peoples of their basic rights.

Nazis, including Hitler, were incredibly outspoken in their anti-Semitism, and many Nazis were far more obvious than their leader about their plans for ridding Germany of Jews. For instance, the Nazi newspaper *Das Schwarze Korps* published the following revealing statement about their goals for the removal of Jews from Germany on November 24, 1938:

> [W]e are now going to have a total solution to the Jewish question. . . . total separation, total segregation! [This] does not only mean the total exclusion of the

> Jews from the German economic system. . . . It means much more! No German can be expected to live under the same roof as Jews. The Jews must [be] made to live in rows or blocks of houses where they can keep to themselves and come into contact with Germans as little as possible. They must be clearly identified. . . . And when we compel the rich Jews to provide for the "poor" . . . which will certainly be necessary, they will all sink together into a pit of criminality. As this happens, we will be faced with the harsh necessity of [destroying] the Jewish underworld, just as we root out criminals from our own orderly state: with fire and sword. The result will be the certain and absolute end of Jewry in Germany; its complete annihilation [destruction]![1]

This quotation makes their plans seem quite straightforward, but many people couldn't bring themselves to believe what was happening.

Paranoia or Prediction?

Before World War II began in 1939, those who sensed the truth about the Nazis' murderous intentions were often dismissed as alarmists. Eleven-year-old Janina Bauman had a plucky great aunt who fit into this category. In the summer of 1937, Aunt Eugenia was the only person Janina knew who seemed truly alarmed about Hitler:

> She was very distressed and sad and always sighed heavily when she spoke about what was going on in Germany. She would lower her voice and give frightened . . . glances around every time she was about to say "Hitler." I developed a sense that "Hitler" was a rude, shameful word and I never used it. Whenever conversation in the sitting room touched upon the future—next holidays, for example, or plans for another

Members of the Sturmabteilung, also known as stormtroopers or brownshirts, marching at the Nuremberg Rally in 1934. Their flags and banners have the swastika sign on them. The swastika was originally associated with religious practices in Southeast Asia, but Nazis adopted the symbol because they linked it to Aryanism and racial hierarchy.

family get-together—Aunt Eugenia would sigh, "First let's survive." I sensed that nobody really believed what she was telling us. Her frightened glances and whispers [the family] would explain away as an obsession of old age or the first symptoms of paranoia [feelings of persecution]. I think we all felt relieved when she went home to Berlin. None of us ever saw her again. She died in a German concentration camp before the war even began.[2]

The Danger of Denial

Many Jews did not take these threats seriously. They thought the Nazis were bluffing in order to put on a threatening display of power, but they were certain that the German people were far too intelligent to put up with the likes of Adolf Hitler for long. Then Germany invaded Poland on September 1, 1939, and those threats began to seem very real. As the Nazis overran Europe with their blitzkrieg, or "lightning war," Jews coped as best they could.

Some held on to hope by refusing to believe that they were in danger. Survivor Norman Feld remembered how his father clung to hope: even though "there was so much talk of the hatred [the Nazis] had for the Jews . . . my father thought they were only rumors and our area would remain safe."[3]

On September 1, 1939, Norman Feld began realizing what was happening:

Nazi tanks in a parade in Warsaw, Poland, after the Nazi invasion of Poland in September 1939.

> [At] 6 A.M. planes flew over the refinery. The radio announced Hitler had invaded Poland. Sirens went off. We would run to the river and hide. It was a block away. Rumors were that we might be gassed so we wore masks for protection just in case.
>
> [My father] thought it would never happen. . . . [E]ven a few weeks before we were made to go to hide out, he had a meeting at our home and he was very nonchalant about it. He said nothing serious would happen, that God would take care of everything for him and his family. It was amazing he could think this way. It was after several times that Germans would come into your home and they would confiscate guns or take valuables or really whatever they pleased. . . .

Lightning War

Blitzkrieg, literally "lightning war," is a form of warfare that was frequently used by the German military in World War II. A traditional German war tactic was to incapacitate the opposing side psychologically by using rapid and forceful attacks to create confusion and shock. After World War I, technology advanced enough that this traditional method could be applied to coordinate ground and air attacks. In a blitzkrieg-style attack, tanks and military aircraft are used to execute a series of forceful and rapid attacks on enemy troops. After the Nazi invasion, the word "blitzkrieg" became popular in the western media to describe the Nazis' usual attack style.

> [Later] we held a family meeting . . . I just listened, frightened. Should we leave or go to the woods? We might die. My father brought out the bible and said we're innocent. So they went to sleep without a solution. . . . The following morning my sister [went to work], but came running home saying, "Run for your lives."[4]

Though Norman's father didn't want to face it, it had become difficult to deny that grave danger was at hand.

Waiting in Disbelief

Ezra BenGershôm was a seventeen-year-old student when World War II began. He and a group of other young people were learning agriculture at a training farm in the German town of Steckelsdorf. They were planning to go to Palestine and help build a new Jewish state in the ancient land of the Jewish people.

At the beginning of the war they expected deliverance:

> When the deliverance would come no one knew; but come it must! . . . On the way to [work] in the mornings, we [talked about] the future. [The discussions] all began with the words "When the war is over . . ." What had to happen in order for the war to come to an end was something we did not even [try] to think about. . . . On another occasion, we talked about what might lie ahead for us if the war were to last for a long time.
>
> I spoke up: "Here at Steckelsdorf . . .we still have a certain amount of freedom of movement. We wouldn't have that in Poland, and we'd starve even worse than we do here. They'll squeeze the last drop of strength out of us, and then. . . ."
>
> [Another student] disagreed: "I tend to think they'll dump us in some remote spot and leave us to our fate."

> I find it impossible to recall those conversations without a shudder. Why were we not moved by the courage of despair to try to do something about getting away? But, you see we did not believe what we were saying ourselves; it was literally beyond our power to imagine.[5]

Secret Signs

Hiding required elaborate planning, dependable helpers, and considerable financial resources. Many Jews could not even think about hiding because they lacked these resources.

Ezra and his friends from the training farm thought about the possibility of hiding, but soon realized that for some of them it just wasn't a viable solution. Ezra explained:

> By March 1942 we [began talking] about . . . going into hiding. . . . What sort of a hiding-place would one need in order to be tolerably comfortable and if necessary even get by for a year or more? . . . The conclusion we came to was this: anyone who did not have an "Aryan" friend who was prepared to bring him food and to make enormous sacrifices for him should not even [think about] going underground.[6]

Ezra's family eventually was able to create a space in which to live secretly, although some members of the family worked in the outside world. They had a system of secret knocks and signals, combined with a fortress-like door that

> served as both bastion and drawbridge, while the spyhole was our watchtower against the persecutors, both uniformed and plain-clothes, with whom Germany teemed. The door, which was double-leaved, consisted

A Star of David on an apartment door in Berlin, Germany, with the word "Jude," meaning Jew, in the center. The Star of David was adopted globally as the symbol of the Jewish community in the late nineteenth century.

> of some fifty square feet of timber; it was fitted with an iron lock and a patent cylinder lock. The two leaves could be fastened together with a heavy iron bolt about two feet long as well as with a guard chain.
>
> Beyond this wooden bulwark lay the hostile outside world. It extended right up to the coat of white paint covering our front door. A stranger who rang the bell might stand there for a long time. . . . The flat would remain as quiet as the grave; no one would open to him.
>
> Only members of the family and friends who knew our secret knock found their way into the fortress. The Star of David posted outside showed visitors that the enclave behind the door did not belong to the hostile world. Once admitted, with the door safely shut behind them, they could speak freely, [though] only in an undertone. Yet that same Star of David also showed how insecure the fortress was, for all its locks and bolts.[7]

The Ghost in the House

On August 12, 1942, the Gershôms' safe hideaway world broke apart. On that day, Ezra's parents were taken away by the Nazis. Ezra and his siblings would never see them again. The three young people, Ezra, Leon, and Toni, remained together. Leon and Toni worked in a munitions factory. Because they helped produce war materials, the Nazis considered them "necessary workers."

Ezra did not have a necessary job, so he had to live in hiding while his siblings went into the outside world:

> I spent the next few months . . . under twenty-four-hour house arrest. Only very occasionally did I slip out into the street. During the day, when Toni and Leon were out at work, I had to maintain complete silence.

> How little experience I had in the art of keeping my existence secret from the world! It was sounds coming through the ceiling from the flat [apartment] above—a chair leg grating, the hum of a vacuum cleaner—that first made me aware of how easily one can give away one's presence. I promptly took off my squeaky leather shoes and stole about the flat on bare or stockinged feet. But that was not the end of it. A door not properly closed snapped shut by itself. The tap in the kitchen [made] a high-pitched whine. Saucepans . . . slipped from my grasp . . .
>
> After a few days I found I could live more or less without making a sound. I had [learned] to stack china plates silently, to fill the bathtub without splashing, to open and close windows while remaining well out of sight behind the net curtains. . . . and to tidy up, sweep up and wash up as carefully and quietly as if the furniture and the dishes had been made of wafer-thin glass.
>
> I became familiar with a great many sounds from the outside world. The hysterical nagging of a neighbour and the beer-sodden mumble of an old man came from the same ground-floor window across the courtyard. . . . I recognised the postman's footsteps when he was still half a flight below our landing. I could tell exactly when the young woman in the flat above us went out and whether the old people she left at home were in the room above our kitchen, above our living-room, or above our hall.[8]

Surviving with No Safe Place to Go

In the Russian town of Rudnya, Brenda Szyr Senders got caught outside during an Einsatzgruppen raid. She would

No Place to Go

Because of the complicated problems that could come up, including finding a suitable place and locating someone who could act as a link to the outside world, hiding was not usually the first choice for Jews seeking safety. Thousands first tried to escape the danger altogether by emigrating to safe countries. Before the war started in 1939, getting out of Germany was not especially difficult.

The problem was finding someplace to go. No country seemed willing to open the floodgates of immigration to thousands of impoverished refugees. The United States and other countries relied on quotas to curb the tide. This limited immigration to a specified number of people per country. Some Jews made the mistake of waiting too long in hopes of a visa, a document that allows its bearer to enter a given country. They joined the thousands of Jews who found themselves at the mercy of the Nazis.

Jews living under Nazi occupation often had to scramble for hiding places at times of immediate danger. When the Germans invaded the Soviet Union in June 1941, Russian Jews faced a new and terrifying danger. The Nazis did not force them into ghettos. Instead, special execution squads called Einsatzgruppen followed the regular army. They had one job: kill all the Jews in the area.

surely have died if not for some unexpected compassion from one of the executioners:

> There was one German who was standing with [his] gun against us and in this sea of hate, this was still a nice human being. . . . He was in his 50's, my father's age at that time, and I remember my . . . [friend] . . . went up close to him. He had the right at that time to kill her, and I stood right behind her. . . . He said, "Oh my God, I have a daughter your age. What are they doing to you?" And he yelled to us and he said . . . "You dummy, run from here. They are going to kill you." The [moment] my mother saw me going behind the barbed wire, she threw my sister over, and she ran behind me. My first instinct was to go to a Christian family we knew over there. We were friends with them. And this [will stand out] in my mind forever. . . . They could hear the shots. They could hear the yells even. I went up to them and I said, "Hide me." She said, "no, I don't have—I'm afraid."[9]

Though denied a hiding place by this friend, Brenda managed to survive the purge. However, hundreds of Jewish men, women, and children did not. The executioners shot them down and dumped their bodies into a mass grave.

For fourteen-year-old Olga Sher, danger came in the form of Gestapo (Nazi security police) jeeps cruising the streets of the Boryslaw ghetto in Poland. The events of that day were fixed in her mind:

> The air is heavy, the tension is palpable, it is silent and there are no people on the sidewalks. We are all at home. A lone Jewish man, who is a translator for the Germans passes by and my father asks him: "Mr. Haendler, what do you think I should do with my family?" He answers: "If I were you, I would hide them." . . . Since my mother

A member of an Einsatzgruppen unit prepares to shoot a Jewish man in the head. The ditch in the foreground is already full of dead bodies. Other soldiers watch in the background.

> and my sister did not yet have [working papers] we decided that they should go to our Polish [non-Jewish] friends . . . until the danger had [passed]. It was a beautiful warm night when I accompanied them to the house where Ewa and her family lived. . . . Walking in silence we crossed a bridge and the fields and narrow streets of the suburbs. Here and there we saw people, who were desperately searching for a safe place, just to survive the next few days. It occurred to me that they resembled mice looking for a hole to hide in.[10]

In Case of Emergency

People who lived in hiding needed a particularly special place in times of grave danger in case their location was compromised. Some of these hideouts-within-hideouts were planned: spaces were made under floorboards, inside hollow walls, in root cellars, anywhere that could be made into a nook to hide in. Others had to make do with any space at hand. Sally Eisner (born Baran) and her brother were hiding with a gentile farmer and his wife:

> One late afternoon, as dusk approached, my brother was chopping wood in front of the house and I was inside glancing out the window. [I saw] three horsemen approaching. . . . With blind instinct I ran outside, grabbed my brother's hand and pulled him inside and pushed him and myself under the huge peasant bed . . . to hide among the boots, shoes, and many other items that were stored there. We crept as far into the corner as we could, pressing our bodies against the wall and each other. . . . We thought this was the end. . . .
>
> We heard the loud bang as [the men] pushed open the door. . . . They started to search the house. . . . Then

> they approached our hiding place. They thrust the bayonets under the bed, sweeping the floor with the blades, stabbing and jabbing into the dark and cluttered space, pulling out boots and shoes. I felt the knife point against my skin but we didn't make a sound. . . . When they were convinced that no one was under the bed, they went outside. They searched for us in the potato cellar too. . . .
>
> We stayed under the bed for a long time after, afraid to come out. When the family came home and we told them what had happened, they immediately told us to leave. It was a bitter cold winter night. We wandered about for days and finally ended up in a labour camp.[11]

Sally Eisner and her brother survived that labor camp. The Russian Army liberated it in March 1944. The rest of their family was dead.

There were many different kinds of hiding, each with its own special dangers and limitations. From Sally Eisner throwing herself under a bed and dodging bayonet thrusts to Ezra BenGershôm's silent life in an apartment, stories of hiding share a common theme: the search for shelter and safety in an unsafe world.

Chapter 2

Safe Spaces and Secret Places

People who became aware of the Nazi danger early on had the time to make careful plans. Many used that time to develop secret shelters, hoping that their foresight would keep them safe, but this advance preparation did not always work. Secret shelters were a good idea in theory, but it was impossible to sever all contact with the outside world. People needed things like food and other necessities, and everyone who chose to hide for the duration either needed to be prepared to go out into the world themselves or have arranged for a gentile or other person to help keep them safe.

Every trip into the outside world was incredibly dangerous, as hiders could be recognized by the wrong people, accidentally draw unwelcome attention, or simply be in the wrong place at the wrong time. Each journey was a potential death trap. Even those who never set foot outside might be betrayed, whether accidentally or on purpose, and helpers not in hiding risked terrible danger themselves because, as you will read in chapter five, it was illegal to

The house where Anne Frank and her family hid is now a famous landmark in Amsterdam. The Franks were concealed in the home's secret annex from June 1942 to August 1944.

help Jews. Nevertheless some people did hide. Many were found out and suffered terribly, but a few survived.

The Story of Anne Frank

The most well known hiding place of the Holocaust was a secret apartment in Amsterdam, Holland, where Anne Frank's family lived in hiding. They had already escaped the Nazis once, coming to Holland as refugees from Germany. By the spring of 1940, Germany had conquered and occupied Holland, and the Franks needed a new survival plan. Anne's father, Otto Frank, made all the arrangements in secret. He did not tell Anne about the plan until July 1942.

In her diary entry for July 5, 1942, Anne wrote about walking with her father in the town square: "Daddy began to talk [about] going into hiding. I asked him why on earth he was beginning to talk of that already. [He told me] . . . we have been taking food, clothes, furniture to other people for more than a year now."[1]

These few words left Anne to wonder where the family would take refuge: "In a town or the country, in a house or a cottage, when, how, where? . . . These were questions I was not allowed to ask, but I couldn't get them out of my mind." Not until the family prepared to leave did Anne get her answers:

> Margot [Anne's sister] and I began to pack some of our most vital belongings into a school satchel. The first thing I put in was this diary, then hair curlers, handkerchiefs, schoolbooks, a comb, old letters; I put in the craziest things with the idea that [we're] going into hiding. But I'm not sorry, memories mean more to me than dresses.[2]

On the day the family left,

We put on heaps of clothes as if we were going to the North Pole, the sole reason being to take clothes with us. No Jew in our situation would have dreamed of going out with a suitcase full of clothing. I had on two vests, three pairs of pants, a dress, on top of that a skirt, jacket, summer coat, two pairs of stockings, lace-up shoes, wooly cap, scarf, and still more. I was nearly stifled before we started, but no one [asked] about that.

Margot filled her satchel with schoolbooks, fetched her bicycle, and rode off . . . into the unknown, as far as I was concerned. You see I still didn't know where our secret hiding place was to be.[3]

Publishing the Diary

Sadly, the only member of the Frank family who survived the war was Anne's father, Otto. Yet Anne lived on through her famous diary, which Miep Gies had rescued from the Secret Annexe and kept safe for years until giving it to Otto Frank after the war ended and Anne's death at Bergen-Belsen had been confirmed. Otto translated the diary into German for his friends and relatives who had survived the war and who tried to convince him it should be published. The first edition was published by a Dutch publishing house in 1947 and sold extremely well. The first English translation of the diary was published by Doubleday in 1952 and quickly became a best seller—readers were captivated by Anne's story and her unique voice. To date, it has been published in over sixty languages.

The Home Within the Office

Anne Frank called her family's hiding place the "Secret Annexe." It was a sectioned-off part of the building where her father had his office. Anne described it in her diary:

> [T]here is a large warehouse on the ground floor which is used as a store. The front door to the house is next to the warehouse door, and inside the front door is a second doorway which leads to a staircase. . . . There is another door at the top of the stairs, with a frosted glass window in it, which has "Office" written in black letters across it. That is the large main office, very big, very light, and very full. . . . A small dark room containing the safe, a wardrobe, and a large cupboard leads to a small somewhat dark second office. Mr. Kraler and Mr. Van Daan used to sit here, now it is only Mr. Kraler. One can reach Kraler's office from the passage, but only via a glass door which can be opened from the inside, but not easily from the outside.
>
> From Kraler's office a long passage goes past the coal store, up four steps and leads to the showroom of the whole building: the private office. Dark, dignified furniture, linoleum and carpets on the floor, radio, smart lamp, everything first class. Next door there is a roomy kitchen with a hot-water faucet and a gas stove. Next door the W.C. [bathroom] That is the first floor.
>
> A wooden staircase leads from the down- stairs passage to the next floor (B). There is a small landing at the top. There is a door at each end of the landing, the left one leading to a storeroom at the front of the house and to the attics. One of those really steep Dutch staircases runs from the side to the other door opening on to the street.

The right-hand door leads to our "Secret Annexe". No one would ever guess that there would be so many rooms hidden behind that plain gray door. There's a little step in front of the door and then you are inside.

There is a steep staircase immediately opposite the entrance. On the left a tiny passage brings you into a room which was to become the Frank family's bed-sitting-room, next door a smaller room. . . . On the right [there was] a little room without windows containing the washbasin and a small W.C. compartment, with

Rachel Shtibel poses with her violin and her husband, Adam, for the Azrieli Series of Holocaust Survivor Memoirs.

> another door leading to Margot's and my room. If you go up the next flight of stairs and open the door, you are simply amazed that there could be such a big light room in such an old house by the canal.[4]

Though eight people lived in the Secret Annexe, it was still reasonably comfortable for all. Four longtime friends who had worked for Mr. Frank kept the hiders supplied and brought them news of the outside world. Still, Anne learned early on that living in hiding would not be easy:

> It is the silence that frightens me so in the evenings and at night. . . . I can't tell you how oppressive it is *never* to be able to go outdoors, also I'm very afraid that we shall be discovered and be shot. That is not exactly a pleasant prospect.
>
> We have to whisper and tread lightly during the day, otherwise the people [working] in the warehouse might hear us.[5]

Like Ezra BenGershôm, the residents of the Secret Annexe had to keep completely silent in order to stay hidden.

Digging in the Dirt

Rachel Shtibel was not yet a teenager when her family took her into hiding. After escaping the Kolomyja ghetto, they took refuge with Vasil and Maria Olehrecky, Polish farmers who had worked for Rachel's grandfather. Their hiding place was a barn with a broken roof. In the winter of 1943, bitter cold and the danger of discovery drove them to leave. They joined other relatives at the farm of another Polish couple, Vasil and Paraska Hapiuk.

Trouble awaited them when they arrived. One day, during a family quarrel, Hapiuk's daughter-in-law threatened to report the Jews living in the barn:

> Uncle Moses convinced Vasil to tell his family that the Jews had left and that it would be their secret that they had stayed. He told Vasil that God would bless him for being so kind. Vasil did not have the heart to turn the Jewish family out to die and so he agreed…
>
> Aunt Mina was worried. "Vasil only knows about the four of us and now there will be ten." My father had a solution. "We must dig a bunker in the ground under the straw that could hold the ten of us." Immediately, the men found some tools in the barn and started digging. They worked through the night and dug what looked like a big grave, three meters by three meters square.
>
> Dark and airless. Our positions were organized in such a way that Uncle Moses could lie near the opening so that Vasil would see only him when he came with food.
>
> Five people lay on one side and the other five on the opposite side. We lay foot to foot—toes touching. Aunt Mina and Luci lay beside Moses. I lay with my parents. And there was Bubbie [grandmother] Yetta and Shiko and Baruch. And Dr. Neider.
>
> In these positions we remained. There was no room for standing or moving. When one person had to turn, all of us would have to turn. The deeper we were inside the bunker, the less air we had. There were strict rules for Luci and me. We were kept apart from each other and were not allowed to use our voices to speak. We could only communicate by moving our lips. Turn. Whisper. Turn.
>
> Sometimes, the adults took pity on us and gave us something important to do. It was our job to wake

> someone by touching them if they were snoring in their sleep, and that was usually Bubbie Yetta. We would giggle at the strange sounds she made and immediately we would be told, "Stop laughing and be quiet. The Germans are coming." The word German was enough and we knew all too well what that meant.[6]

Rachel and her parents survived the war with the help of Russian soldiers who liberated eastern Poland. The family returned to Kolomyja when both the Germans and the ghetto were gone. They eventually emigrated to Canada, where they built a new life.

The Inspection

In the Polish town of Kosowa, Jews did not sense their immediate danger. It was the summer of 1941, and the Nazis had not yet occupied the town. They camped a few miles away, giving the townsfolk a false sense of security. One day, they ordered all Jewish men between the ages of eighteen and sixty to assemble for "inspection."

Teenager Bronia Beker would never forget that day:

> My three brothers went but my father, who was exactly 60, did not. The Nazis selected 300 [of the men], including two of my . . . brothers, led them to the nearby forest and shot them all...
>
> Soon after this horrible event our ghetto was established. Since my parents had a big house, all of us, ten people, moved in, to be together. By this time the Nazis started their random killings. Every time they entered our town, whenever they caught any Jews on the streets, they just killed them on the spot.[7]

The ghetto of Lublin, Poland, housed many Polish Jews as well as a number of Romani people. It was one of the first ghettos to be scheduled for liquidation, and in the spring of 1942, tens of thousands of Jewish residents were sent from Lublin to death camps.

The family did not have the resources to leave the ghetto. Their only chance for survival was making a hiding place within it:

> We [Jews in the ghetto] started to build bunkers and other hiding places in our homes. In our own home with the help of a few remaining strong men, we dug a very big cave in the ground, about 12 x 6 feet. Deep enough so an adult could stand up. [We] covered it on top with some kind of a trap door and two pipes were installed in one corner, for air circulation. Frequently, all ten of us had to spend hours there. Sometimes we stood in there a whole day, when the Nazis came and were looking for people to kill. We heard them walking around upstairs and only when we were sure they left would we come out of the cave.
>
> One night [in] April 1941. . . . We heard from others that the Germans [had]
>
> surrounded the town and the next day would liquidate the ghetto. . . . we all went into . . . the cave. . . .
>
> In the morning we heard the Nazis walking upstairs, shouting and yelling, looking for us. While they didn't find the entrance to the cave they must have spotted the two air pipes sticking out. They stuffed them with something and thus blocked the flow of air. I was the first to faint. I was weak anyway because I just recently recovered from typhus. . . . I didn't know about anything until later. . . .
>
> When the Germans finally left, [my aunt] came to our house to see what had happened. When she didn't see or hear anyone answering her calls, she became frightened. She went to look for the few remaining people in the ghetto. They came to the cave, opened the trap door and pulled us out, one by one. Later they told

> me that everyone was dead, suffocated. . . . They noticed that my eye- lids started to flutter, so they poured cold water on me and I revived. . . . That day the Nazis killed 1,000 Kozowa Jews.[8]

Living and Dying in the Walls

In September 1942, the Nazis began liquidating the ghetto in Sokolow-Podlaski, Poland, where ten-year-old Aaron Elster lived with his family. Desperate for any sort of hiding place, the Elster family and several of their neighbors had to take refuge inside a double wall:

> It is very scary [behind the wall]. I can't stop thinking of death and pain, the pain that comes with death. The [Nazis] find us quickly and rip open the wall. The SS [starts] shooting into our hiding place. People are dying around me, bleeding and dying. I know these people, they are not bad people, they have done nothing wrong, they are like me. . . . We are dragged out of our hiding place. They scream at us, "Out you dirty Jews!" We run out of our hiding place into the street. . . . I am terrified, [too] scared to even look up. I cannot control my fears and my whole body starts to shake, but I don't cry. I guess I think that if I don't look up in their faces they won't see me. Every where I look, people are screaming and being shot. People are being dragged out of their houses, beaten, clubbed and chased to the back of their homes where they are shot and thrown into a mass grave. . . . The people that are left are pushed and shoved into a line, and then marched into the train that will take them to Treblinka [a Nazi death camp in Poland].[9]

Aaron survived the destruction of the ghetto and eventually made his way to a Polish family that had sheltered his sister. They did not want him:

> When [Mrs. Gurski] sees me she is angry and yells at me for coming. She tells me that I am dangerous because if the Germans find out they are helping Jews they will kill them. She tells me that my sister isn't here anymore and she wants me to leave right now. I beg and cry for her to let me hide in her attic, even if only for a little

Abandoned and Alone

Magda Denes felt abandoned when her mother left her in a children's shelter. It was for the best, her mother claimed. Vadasz Utca was not very nice and was far too dangerous for children. The people there operated a rescue project, helping Jews get out of Hungary and into safe hiding.

No matter how much Magda pleaded, her mother held firm. Magda would be safe at the center, she promised, but that turned out to be wrong. Life at the center turned upside down when the caretakers heard that the Germans knew where the children were hiding. They could come at any time, killing some people, taking the rest somewhere to work or to die.

Magda wrote a desperate letter to her mother, begging her to come get her, but her mother refused to allow Magda to join her in Vadasz Utca. Magda spent the rest of the war living in a dark attic above a bakery shop.

while. I guess because I look really sick and because I am begging for help she let me stay in the attic, finally agrees to but only for a few days and that I must leave after that.

A few days later my sister appears, she is allowed to come into the attic with some hot water so that I can wash. I am full with lice and other kind of crawly stuff. The Gurskis give me a pail to use as a toilet and once a day, but not knowing when, Mrs. Gurski or my sister bring me some soup and a slice of bread. Those few days turn into weeks and those weeks eventually turn into years. I live in that attic for nearly 2 years.

My days in the attic are spent in fear of being discovered. . . . My days and nights are also very lonely. I have to be silent, I can't make noise, because I might be discovered by the Germans. I sit in silence, no friends to play with except . . . when it rains.

Rain becomes my good friend, because when it rains, the rain makes such loud noise against the tin roof, that I am able to scream, cry and even sing. This lets whatever is pent up in me come out.[10]

The Right Time to Go

Caution alone could not guarantee safety in hiding. Sometimes survival depended on being alert to signs of grave danger. Norman Feld discovered this while hiding on a farm, working for a Polish family that did not know he was Jewish.

After a time, he became friends with the farmer's son:

[One night] when I was almost asleep, [he] uncovered me and checked to see if I was circumcised. . . . I pretended to be asleep. The next morning, we ate breakfast as usual. Around 10:00 A.M. . . . . he suggested going for

Anne Frank was born in 1929 in Germany and moved with her family to the Netherlands four years later. Her family was largely spared the persecution that Jews in Germany faced in the early years of Hitler's reign, but after Nazis invaded the Netherlands in 1940, the Franks' situation became far more dangerous. This picture is from 1941, the year before the Frank family went into hiding.

a ride. . . . I went to get the fancy buggy and as I was cleaning the horses I looked through the holes in the barn and saw he had a rifle. I was scared, but somehow I didn't run, but I should have. He put the rifle in the buggy . . . and covered it with hay. We took off and went quite a way, [when] I saw that we were going a different direction down a big hill.

I thought he was taking me to the Germans. I had to escape. I saw a creek at the bottom of the hill. I was surprised he didn't just stop and tie me up and shoot me. So . . . I took the leashes of the horses and smacked them and they took off fast. [At the same time], I jumped off and, barefooted, started running. I was already down the hill. I jumped the creek. It was 20 feet minimum. To this day I don't know how I jumped it. So he started shooting and I kept running. . . . into the woods. I climbed up a tree and hid. He couldn'tbget over the creek so somehow he decided to go back.[11]

The End of the Annexe

A completely safe hiding place did not exist during the Holocaust. Even Anne Frank and her family were eventually discovered, probably because someone had reported the odd comings and goings of Miep Gies and other helpers.

In what turned out to be her last diary entry, Anne reflected on herself and her situation:

I have a dual personality. One half contains my exuberant cheerfulness, making fun of everything, my high-spiritedness, above all, the way I take everything lightly. . . .

I'm awfully scared that people who know me as I always am will discover I have another side, a finer and better side. I'm afraid they'll laugh at me, think

> I'm ridiculous and sentimental, not take me seriously. I'm used to not being taken seriously, but it's only the "lighthearted" Anne that's used to it and can bear it; the "deeper" Anne is too frail. . . . [I] keep trying to find a way of becoming what I would so like to be, and what I could be if . . . there were no other people living in the world.[12]

Anne wrote that diary entry on Tuesday, August 1, 1944. On the morning of August 4, a Nazi officer and three members of the Dutch security police broke into the Secret Annexe and arrested everyone inside. They sent the Frank and Van Daan families to Westerbork, a transit camp in Holland. Anne and her sister, Margot, eventually ended up in the Bergen-Belsen concentration camp, where they both died in a typhus epidemic. Anne's father, Otto, survived, and when Miep Gies revealed that she had held onto Anne's diary, Otto decided to get it published. Anne Frank's diary became hugely influential, and Anne herself became an icon of hope in the face of terrible danger.

In spite of the risks of physical hiding, it offered the best chance of survival for many people. Unlike the Franks, many Jews moved from one hiding place to another as conditions changed. In the end, the circumstances of hiding did not matter. Regardless of where they hid, how long they remained, and whether or not they got captured, those who survived were grateful for their lives.

Chapter 3

In Plain Sight

Although Nazis insisted that there was such thing as a Jewish or an Aryan race, it was sometimes impossible to tell who was Jewish and who was not. In fact, race in general is considered a social construct because it has no basis in genetics. Some Jews living in the Holocaust used that fact to their advantage and assumed false, non-Jewish identities.

They learned to look and behave like Aryans: they spoke with a specific accent, learned how to behave during church services, and creating a new identity that would make Nazis overlook them. They often had to move far away from home so that no one would recognize them, and they had to react quickly in difficult situations in order to avoid giving away their Jewish upbringing.

Desperate parents handed their children over to non-Jewish families who gave them false identities and taught them how to behave as Christians. No agency helped make these placements; nobody advertised their willingness to take in Jewish children. To find a suitable place, parents had to rely upon friends, friends of friends, and sometimes even strangers. This separation was traumatic for everyone involved, but parents that did so believed that it was the only way to keep their children safe.

A Good Catholic

Anita Ekstein was not yet a teenager when her father sent her to a gentile home. He began looking for a suitable place in October 1942, just days after his wife got caught in an SS (secret police) roundup:

The Idea of the Aryan

Throughout history, people have used scientific terms and ideas to support their prejudices, often convincing themselves that a person with certain physical or cultural characteristics is somehow less intelligent or capable than they are, even when such a belief is illogical. Nazified schools and Nazi propaganda used inaccurate biological ideas about race to promote anti-Semitic and racist beliefs. Nazi biology used irrelevant details like head shape and profile to claim that the "Aryan race," meaning the group of white Europeans of Germanic and Nordic descent, was superior to all others. They divided humans into different races based on arbitrary physical attributes and ranked these races, placing Aryans at the top and Jews, Poles, Russians, and Africans at the bottom in a category labeled "untermeschen" or "subhuman." Today we understand that race is a socially create concept and that racial categories are rarely useful or accurate on a scientific, biological level.

> I remember . . . waking up [to see] my father sitting beside my bed, crying and telling me that my mother was gone and that we won't know when we would see her again. . . . [Later] we learned that this particular transport was taken to Belzec [a death camp]. I believe this is where the Nazis killed my mother. The date was October 18, 1942.
>
> Afterwards, my father seemed to have lost the will to live. He was working and taking care of me. . . . [At work] he met a Pole by the name of Jozef Matusiewicz. . . . [Mr. Matusiewicz] and my father became friends and one day my father asked him if he would save his little girl.
>
> Mr. Matusiewicz was a wonderful man. . . . He smuggled me out of the ghetto in Skole and took me to his home in Rozdol. . . . I was supposed to be an orphaned niece, whose parents had died in a flu epidemic. I was given a new name which I had to memorize and always remember. I became Anna Jaworska.[1]

Even with forged identity papers, a good cover story, and an Aryan appearance, there were cultural differences to overcome. Even the youngest hidden children had to learn how to behave like gentiles. In devout Catholic homes, they had to learn how to behave in church. They also had to be ready for any unexpected questions from suspicious Nazis.

Anita Ekstein's foster family, the Matusiewiczs, were devout Catholics. They kept Anita hidden from the outside world while she learned the things she needed to know:

> This was a very religious family and they started teaching me how to be a good Catholic. This was necessary so I would be prepared to answer any questions, if asked,

> and this would also be safer for me and for the family. . . . I was kept in the house and had to disappear when someone knocked, that is until I was ready to meet others. Of course I did not go to school. Lusia, the 18-year-old daughter of the family . . . taught me how to read and write at home.

Anita was too young to understand the importance of learning how to behave until one day in February or March of 1943:

> [We] were sitting in the front room reading and we saw two soldiers with rifles walk by the window and knock at the front door. . . . Lusia ran with me to . . . the back of the house and pushed me out of the window. It was winter and there was a lot of snow. I was not dressed for outdoors, but I ran and hid. . . . I stayed [hidden] until it was dark, and then I crept back to the house.

That night, Anita heard some strange sounds that she did not understand: "The following day we found out. A few Jews were discovered still hiding in Rozdol. They were lined up in the cemetery and were shot—one by one. That would have been my fate too had they found me that day."[2] After that, Anita redoubled her efforts to pass as a Catholic.

The Savior at City Hall

Like Anita Ekstein, young people with false identity papers had the best chance of maintaining their Aryan identity, because it made their new, safer identity more official. If they were ever stopped and questioned, papers could be the difference between life and death. During the war, skilled forgers made a business of supplying these documents.

Magda Lipner had a school friend whose father was a Notary Public and dealt with all kinds of official

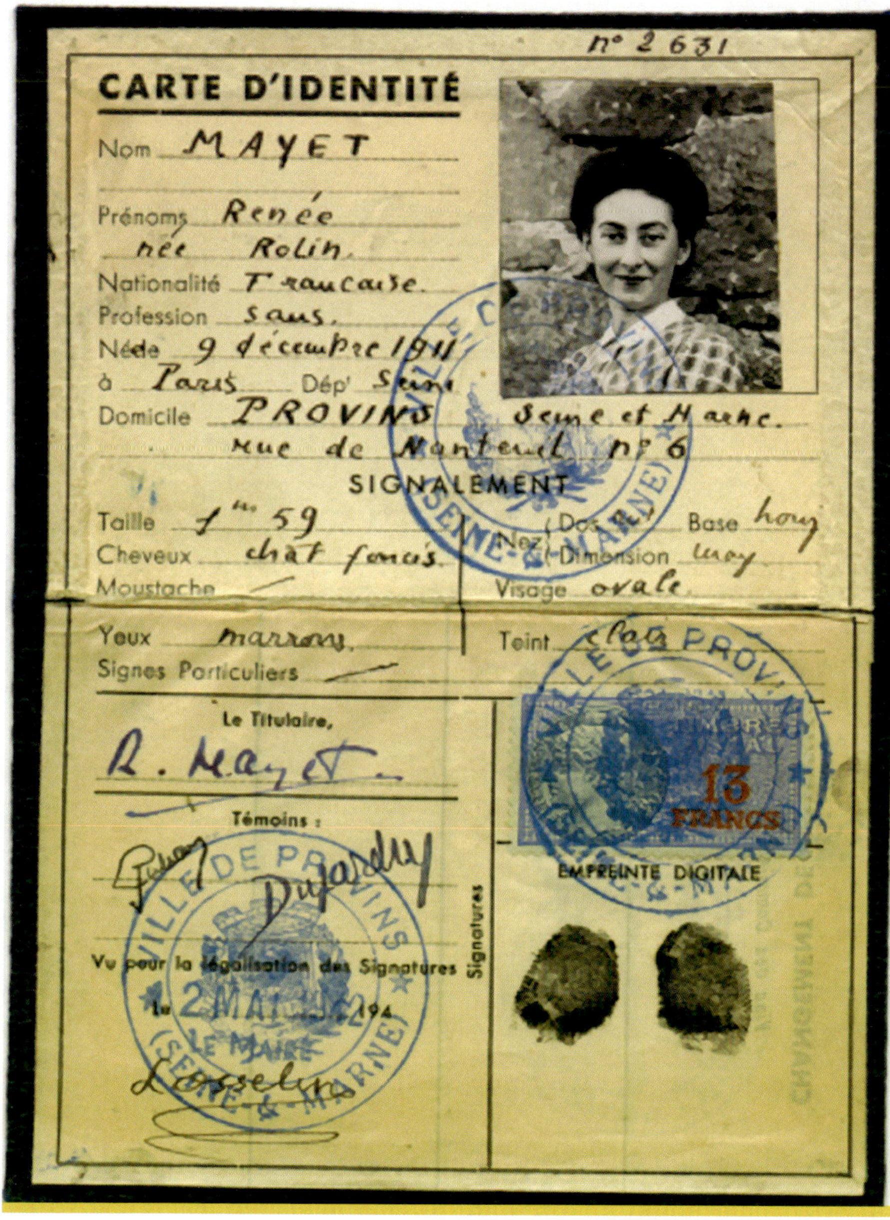
n° 2631

CARTE D'IDENTITÉ

Nom MAYET

Prénoms Renée

née Rolin

Nationalité Française

Profession sans

Née le 9 décembre 1911

à Paris Dép' Seine

Domicile PROVINS Seine et Marne

rue de Nanteuil n° 6

SIGNALEMENT

Taille 1m 59 | Dos | Base

Cheveux chât foncés | Nez | Dimension moy

Moustache — | Visage ovale

Yeux marrons | Teint clair

Signes Particuliers —

Le Titulaire,

R. Mayet

Témoins :

Dujardin

Vu pour la légalisation des Signatures

le 2 MAI 194

Le Maire

Signatures

13 FRANCS

EMPREINTE DIGITALE

VILLE DE PROVINS (SEINE-&-MARNE)

In order to travel in Aryan neighborhoods without arousing suspicion, Jews needed false papers listing Gentile-sounding names. These false papers belonged to Renée Kohn-Mayer, listing her name as Renée Mayet.

documents: "He prepared [a] Birth Certificate, [writing it out] with Chinese ink so it should look old. He pasted the necessary stamps on it . . . he took them off from an old document. This Birth Certificate was written with an excellent handwriting, it really looked authentic. It was a great document, and it saved my life."[3]

False documents also saved Anita Magnus Frank and her siblings. When the Germans occupied the Netherlands, the Magnus family found help at City Hall in the town of Breda:

> [A] man who worked at City Hall . . . knew what was going to happen to us . . . he came to my father's house and he basically said do you want to be killed . . . if I promise to help you, will you try and get out. . . . Other Dutch friends had given us names of people who were willing to take in Jewish children, and within a week we disappeared. . . . [It] turned out to be just in time, just before the [whole] family would have been deported to Auschwicz. . . . [This man] gave us authentic passports—because he had access to the blanks.

Even with good papers, the journey to safety became a very frightening ordeal for Anita Magnus Frank and her brother:

> [We] were taken away . . . to a family in the same town we lived in, and we stayed there for two weeks. Several families would live in the same house, so we lived on the second floor of this house and there [was] another family living on the first floor. [They] did not know that we were on the second floor. So for two weeks we could not move. I remember we slept in the bathtub. . . . We couldn't do anything because . . . [if] the people downstairs would find out that we were upstairs we'd be

> killed. . . . We had no idea where our parents were. . . . and yet we knew . . . there was no crying. There was no whining. There was just obedience.[4]

The Magnus children ended up living with a family that owned a small private school: "[B]ecause they ran a school, they took in other children who were not Jewish and so for them to have other children . . . was not as obvious as it would have been for . . . an ordinary family. So that was a very safe place for us to be. . . . [We] were told never ever, ever to tell anybody we were Jewish."[5]

Except for hiding their Jewish identity, Anita Magnus and her brother lived in relative comfort:

> We were able to go to school. . . . We had friends. We could play, breathe fresh air and yet I . . . knew that I could be betrayed at any time, and so I learned early in the game that I was not to draw any attention to myself. . . . I had to be a very good girl. I could not be naughty. I could not do anything that would make anybody notice me. And so I learned not to complain and I learned not to express any feelings. . . . I didn't dare do anything that . . . would make people angry at me because if they were angry at me they might betray me.[6]

Stranger in a Strange Land

Like Anita Magnus, most young people living under false identities learned to tread carefully. Those who were not comfortable with their Aryan identities lived in a constant state of fear. Raszka Galek found an interesting way to deal with this problem. After getting false papers as a Polish Catholic girl named Maria Kowalciza, she volunteered to work in Germany.

Some people may have considered this a foolish choice, but Raszka felt certain that she would be safer there than in Poland, because in Germany she would be a foreigner, so people would not expect her to behave like them, speak like them, or know little details of the culture. The Germans even gave her a choice of where to work: on a farm, in a factory, or in a hotel. She chose a farm:

> I knew it [would be] a lot of hard work but I [wouldn't] meet so many Poles. I was afraid to meet Poles. . . . Okay. I was a city girl. I never knew . . . what work means because at home we were wealthy. We had maids, and . . . we had everything. I never even knew how to boil a glass of water. Very spoiled . . . well taken care of, and I had no idea what a farm means . . . work on a farm. Anyway, but I adapted and adjusted very well. I knew that that's the way it is. That's the way it's going to be. I better make the best of it.[7]

Among Anti-Semites

When faced with leaving home, Magda Lipner decided to go to Budapest, Hungary, and look for a job. She took a train to the city, taking care that nothing she said, did, or carried would make her stand out in the crowd:

> I had only a small school bag in my hand, and a double skirt on. [I carried] a newspaper published by the Nazi party. . . . While [I was] waiting [at the station] two persons with suitcases were arrested and led away [by] the Hungarian authorities. . . .
>
> [In Budapest], I [looked] for a furnished room. There was another girl also looking for a room . . . so we [teamed up] and [rented a place]. . . . I found [work]

in a big factory, which made rifles and other arms for the army.[8]

Even with a job and a Polish name, Magda Lipner still encountered many dangers. She and her roommate soon learned that their living quarters were not completely safe: "Our landlady was a very big Nazi party member, if she would find out about us, we would be in . . . big danger. There was a son in the family, about seventeen or eighteen, one day he came home with hand grenades in his belt. We were [horrified] and had to . . . [pretend] friendliness toward him."[9]

Somehow Magda managed to handle these situations. She survived the war working in a munitions factory, but

The Vichy Government

With Britain, France declared war on Germany in 1939, when the Nazis first invaded Poland, but French and British forces were unable to stand against the German military. Britain was forced off the European continent, and northern France fell under Nazi control in 1940. The southern part of France was nominally free, but it was effectively an agent of the Nazi German government. Since the capital of France, Paris, was under German military control, Vichy became the capital of the unoccupied region of the south, and southern France became known as Vichy France. Due to Nazi influence, the Vichy government set about arresting all foreign Jews and sending them to detention camps throughout France.

In 1942, workers in a munitions factory in Germany inspect shells needed for the war effort.

the rest of her family did not fare so well. Her parents and two brothers died in the camps, leaving Magda, her sister, and a young niece as the only surviving members of their family.

A Narrow Escape

Danger could come from anywhere and from any source. The ability to recognize that danger could be a matter of life and death. Ruth Kapp Hartz lived in Vichy France, where a puppet government supported the Nazis. Relatives gave her a new name: Renée. Living under a false identity soon taught Renée to think before trusting anyone. That habit may have saved her when she met a stranger on the way home from school:

> [Just] as I reached the street light at the corner, a woman comes out of a doorway and blocks my way. I recognize her, but I can't remember her name. Her face scares me. How does she know me?
>
> "Well now, I've been waiting for you, little Renée," she says. "Where are you going in such a hurry?"
>
> "Home," I tell her.
>
> She calls me by the French name that Jeannette [a cousin] gave me when she first took me to school in Toulouse. At home, I am still called Ruth; but in public, everyone must think I am French. . . .
>
> "Where do you live?" the lady asks.
>
> I look down at her black shoes and shake my head. "I forget the name of the street," I tell her. I am forbidden to tell anyone where we live, even my friends at school. [Mother] says it is too dangerous to tell anyone. The woman is staring at me. She is an old lady with grey

hair and a fat stomach. . . . She has the face of a mean woman, someone you can't trust.

"How can you be on your way home, if you don't know what street you live on?" she asks. Her face is lined. There's a deep furrow between her brows.

"Where is Jeannette today?"

I'm confused. I shake my head. Suddenly, I remember where I have seen the lady before. She works at school, in the office. I make up a lie. "I have to go to my friend's house. . . . she lives up there." I point far up the street to where it narrows around a bend. "Papa comes to pick me up when his shift is over." My voice is shaky. I swallow several times. Maybe I shouldn't have mentioned Papa. Now she knows he does shift work somewhere in the city.

The woman looks up the street in the direction I am pointing. Then she tries to take my arm, as if she is about to lead me somewhere. Just as her hand touches the sleeve of my sweater, I dart around the corner. I run into a café and hide just inside the door for a long time.[10]

A Starring Role

The first rule of survival for Jews living as Aryans was not to attract any attention. However, sometimes Jewish young people had to ignore that rule. Many survivors owed their lives to some outrageous action.

With little more than determination and good identity papers, Barbara Ledermann Rodbell went on tour with a Dutch ballet company. It was a public existence, made all the more dangerous by Barbara's underground activities.

The Jewish resistance in Amsterdam, Holland, approved the idea, largely because touring theatrical companies were exempt from curfew laws:

> And that way I could help shift people from one hiding place to another. . . . let me tell you how this was done. [There] were no more taxis, there were very few cars because there was no gasoline. . . . So what they had was people on bicycles pulling . . . little wagons behind them. . . . [The people] that I moved were moved in the middle of the night . . . after curfew, with them being [bent down] and me . . . sitting on their backs, [wearing] a rather short skirt . . . with makeup on still from the ballet. And when the Germans [said] "What is this? Curfew is on." . . . I would have a smile and papers.[11]

Barbara never got used to these inspections, but she was always ready for them. There was no way to prepare for unexpected dangers. They came out of nowhere, demanding immediate action. This happened to twelve-year-old Yehuda Nir when he tried to reach his aunt's apartment on the Aryan side of Warsaw:

> Alone and numb with fear, I walked through the city streets to Sonia's apartment.
>
> By then, we were not allowed to leave the ghetto without special permits, so I took off my Star of David. . . . My heart was pounding. I wanted to run, but I knew it could be suicidal; [the Nazis] would easily spot a running Jew. I decided to skip, moving rapidly yet merging with the many children happily playing in the park. This was the first of many on-the-spot role changes I would make when faced with [immediate] danger. I was developing the skills of a chameleon, and

Barbara Ledermann was a childhood friend of Anne Frank who, unlike Frank, managed to escape the Nazis in the Netherlands. In this 1960 image, she stands in front of a theater where the film version of Anne Frank's diary is playing.

it felt better, safer. I added whistling to my skipping, and the image was complete.[11]

What Does a Jew Look Like?

Yehuda, along with his mother and sister, had recently moved from their home in Lwów to Krakow, Poland, where they would be strangers, but even this was not safe enough for Yehuda, who did not look at all like a Pole:

> Mother and Lala were very concerned about my looks. I was too pale. It was the height of the summer, and everyone around us was tanned. They said my hair was too dark. Lala wanted me to smile more. Ludwig [a family friend] thought my posture wasn't right; I should walk with my chin up. I knew I was in trouble. They didn't think I looked Aryan.[12]

Two bottles of peroxide turned Yehuda's dark hair blond, but that "was not the image of the Polish boy we all had in mind. . . . we decided that . . . I would avoid going out on the street and would stay at home wherever we were going to be."[13]

After the family found lodging, Lala and her friend Marysia "passed" as Poles so they could look for jobs as maids. The girls moved freely in and out of the room, while Yehuda remained in hiding:

> The days seemed endless, with nothing to break the . . . silence. I imagined that this must be how one felt in jail carrying a life sentence. I seemed to have been sentenced to this kind of penal existence merely for being a Jew.
>
> I spent my days standing behind the curtain at the window, looking at what little action took place on the street.[14]

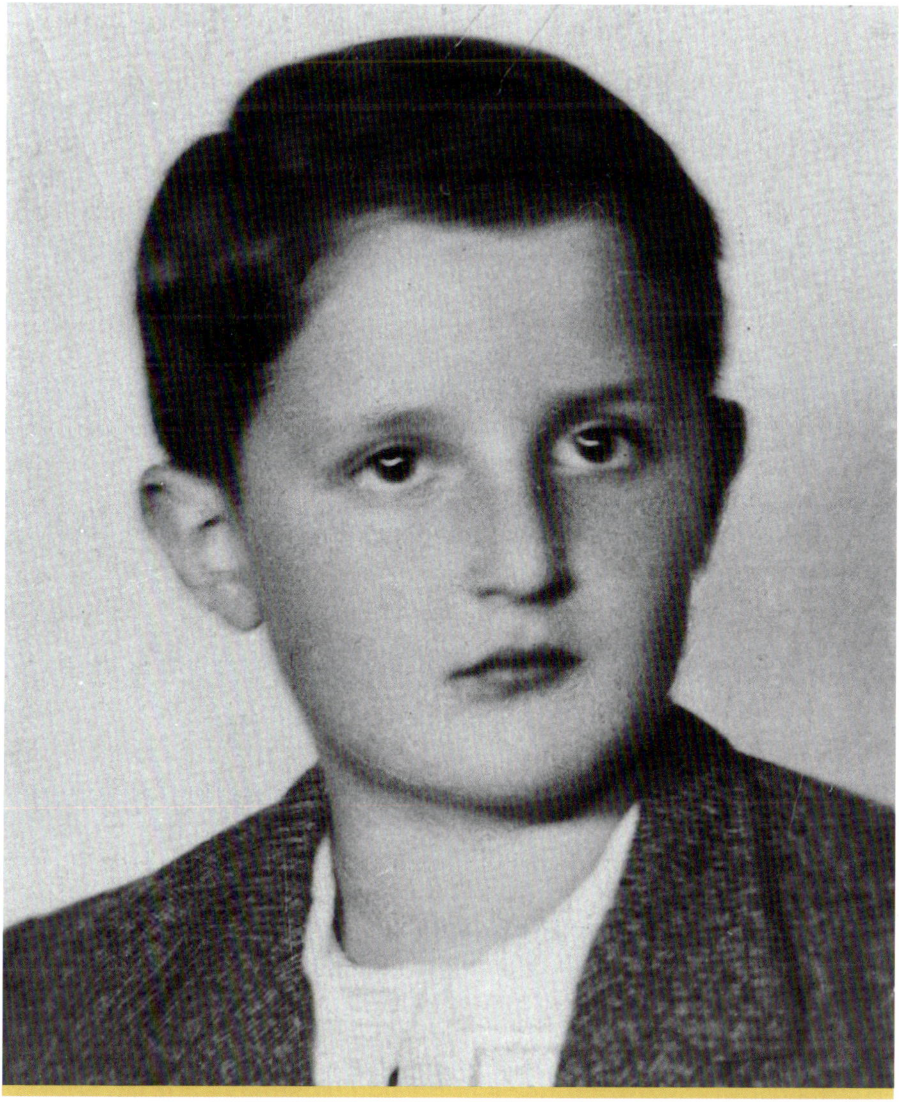

Yehuda Nir was nine years old in 1939. In 1941, Nir's father was murdered in a violent riot where angry Ukrainians were encouraged by German soldiers to kill Jewish members of their community. Soon after, Nir's sister's boyfriend was able to secure false papers for the family, and Nir survived the war by pretending not to be Jewish.

Yehuda Nir never felt safe in hiding. He always worried that someone might have noticed a boy moving in with his mother, never to be seen again. There was no way to know until a young married couple moved into the building:

> [They were] surprised to find that I lived there, having been told by our landlord . . . that the rooms on our floor were rented to two women. This was good news; it meant that downstairs [in the landlord's apartment] they did not know of my existence. Still, because of my circumcision, I continued to be the most vulnerable member of our trio.[15]

A Slip of the Tongue

Young people hiding behind false identities lived in constant fear of exposure. There was no telling when or how it might come. For all his cleverness, Yehuda Nir made a blunder that almost cost him his life. Until then, false identity papers and quick thinking had served him well. When he was thirteen, he found a job as an errand boy and all-around helper to a dentist on the Aryan side of Warsaw.

Christine, the doctor's young dental assistant, took him into her confidence. She talked a great deal about her boyfriend and hinted at other romantic exploits as well:

> In November I nearly caused a disaster. [Christine and I] were discussing the forthcoming Christmas holiday. I, in my ignorance of Christian holidays, remembering that Easter came late in 1943, asked, "On what date does Christmas fall this year?"
>
> She looked at me in complete disbelief. I sensed immediately that I had asked the wrong question. It was too late, however. She hesitated for a second and then said suspiciously, "So you don't know when Christmas

is? You must then be a Jew! That makes sense. . . . Now I know why you knew more German than I did; *All* Jews are international cosmopolitans. You run the Kremlin and Wall Street."

Denying the truth would [not work]: I was at her mercy. . . . She must have been very upset about having confided all the [details] of her life to me. She wasn't talking to me anymore. . . . I knew I had only twenty minutes before Dr. Brabetz returned. Those twenty minutes would determine whether or not I survived. I had to act swiftly.

I made my decision. I went over to Christine and with all my strength, hit her in the face. She was taken by surprise. I had scared her. "Now shut up!" I said. "I know you can report me, but . . . if you do it your life will be over too. I'm going to write to [your boyfriend] about your affair with the old man. I will also tell Dr. Brabetz that you have been sleeping with her fiancé." . . .

[S]uddenly . . . our roles were reversed. Christine looked panic-stricken. She grabbed my hand and started to plead. . . .

"I will be silent if you will" [I said]. I knew now that I was on top of the situation. She didn't say a word, just nodded her head.[17]

Red in the Light

Unlike Yehuda Nir, Leah Hammerstein Silverstein did nothing to give herself away. She was almost betrayed because the color of her hair was common among European Jews. She saved herself by remembering to play her part as a gentile girl: "I was sitting in front of a big basket [cleaning vegetables] and the sun rays came on my head and one of the girls said, 'Look her hair is reddish, like a Jewess' [a female Jew]. And everybody laughed and I laughed most hilariously . . . [but] the fear was gnawing on my insides."

Playing the part saved her again when a cook played a practical joke:

> [He] grabbed me and put my head on the table. He was preparing the . . . sausage for the evening supper. And he put this long knife to my neck and said, "You see, if you were Jewish, I would cut off your head." Big laughter in the room, and I laughed most hilariously, of course. But [do] you know what it does to . . . a young girl in her formative years? Can you imagine? With nobody to . . . console you, with nobody to tell you it's okay, it'll be better, hold on. Total isolation, total loneliness. It's a terrible feeling. . . . You are among people and you are like on an island all alone. There is nobody you can go to ask for help. . . . [or] for advice. You had to make life- threatening decisions all by yourself in a very short time, and you never knew whether your decision will be [helpful] to you or [threaten] your existence. . . . And it was not only one incident. It was [that] way from the moment I came on the Aryan side.[18]

A Perilous Party

David Landau was only thirteen when Adolf Hitler came to power in Germany. He grew to adulthood in a troubled and violent world, learning the lessons of survival that would carry him through the Holocaust. For all his nerve and knowledge, he almost lost his cover over a birthday party:

> I recall an incident when, in a matter of less than three minutes, I endangered the lives of our [Polish] friends Jurek and Zosia and probably also the life of Luba. In

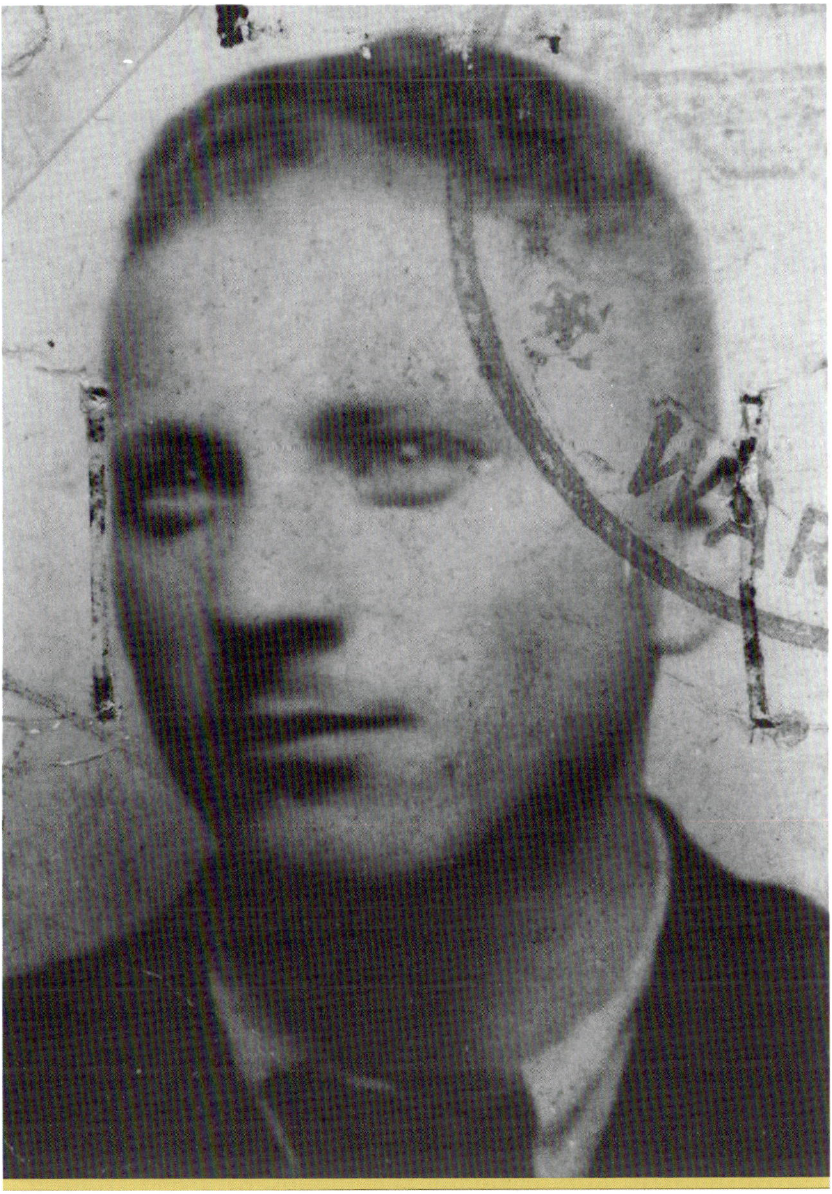

This photo appeared on the false identification card of Benjamin Meed (born Benjamin Miedzyrzecki), a member of the Polish-Jewish underground. He helped people move in and out of the Warsaw ghetto in the early 1940s.

normal times, the incident would have hardly [been worth] a mention. The Polish people rarely celebrate a birthday; the individual celebrates on the day of the Saint by the same name. Jurek and I, Janek [David's false Polish name], celebrated our Name's Day on 24 July. During wartime, when Poles had so little to celebrate, the Name's Day became a good occasion for festivities with friends. . . . On July 24, 1943 I went to meet with Zygmunt, who had some identity documents for me. As a Jew I did not know that this was the day when all Jureks, Jasneks, and Jasieks celebrated. Zygmunt, although a native Pole, obviously gave it no thought. . . .

Zygmunt gave me the documents and I made my way home. I pressed on the door-handle, then realized that I should have knocked or rung the bell, as the door was always locked to give us time to move into the kitchen—but the door opened! An army of eyes turned on me. . . . [Around the table] sat twenty guests partaking in a huge festive feast. I did not know what the occasion was but knew that I had better catch the festive mood quickly; but first I had to know what was being celebrated.

I might have gotten away with it if Zosia, who was always slightly dangerous when tipsy, had not called out: "Ah, Jasio, you are just in time to celebrate with us Jurek's Name's Day." The moment she said it her face changed. . . . If I was Jasio it was also my own Name's Day, and obviously I should have been at my own celebration. None of the guests knew me and I knew nobody. . . . When Zosia mentioned the reason for the celebration it threw me for just long enough to give me away, as somebody who could not be what he appeared to be.[19]

Zosia stepped in quickly, saving the day by telling her guests the "secret" about this stranger: he was a member of the Polish underground, hiding in the forest and fighting Germans. Taking his cue from her, David played the role of a Polish patriot long enough to save the situation.

Close calls like this were normal for Jews living under assumed identities. Any one of them could spell disaster. In spite of the danger, teens and even young children found the strength to cope. Regardless of the outcome, that effort alone was an act of courage.

Chapter 4

Protectors and Persecution

People who protected Jews were subject to many of the same tortures and punishments faced by Jews themselves, up to and including death. Yet many incredibly courageous people continued to help Jews stay safe. Some acted out of moral obligation, friendship, or both while others did it unwillingly, because a spouse or other family member brought Jews into their home. Still others did it for money or compensation.

Whatever the reason, aiding Jews had grave consequences, and protectors often dealt with sever fear and paranoia. The threat of being found out was always present, and it was almost impossible to know who to trust. A close friend or even family member might cave to Nazi pressure or seek out some reward and betray the helper, or they could simply come under suspicion. Even those who helped unwillingly showed great courage in resisting the Nazi regime.

The Kindness of Miep Gies

Miep Gies was a longtime employee of Otto Frank's business and a gentile who kept Anne Frank and her family supplied with necessities in their Secret Annexe. In doing so, she took a tremendous risk, but she acted out of friendship and loyalty. She had a special fondness for Anne because she knew what it was like to grow up in dangerous times and to be dependent on the kindness of strangers. After World War I, eleven-year-old Miep was sent away from her parents in Austria:

> I was not the strongest child, and because of the serious food shortages during the war, I had become undernourished and sick. I was a small child to begin with, and seemed to be wasting away, rather than growing normally. My legs were sticks dominated

Miep Gies at an exhibit honoring Anne Frank and her family, titled *Die Welt der Anne Frank*, or *The World of Anne Frank*, in 1995.

> by bony kneecaps. My teeth were soft. When I was ten years old, my parents had another child; another daughter. Now there was even less food for us all. My condition was worsening, and my parents were told that something had to be done or I would die.
>
> Because of a program that had been set up by foreign working people for hungry Austrian children, a plan was devised that might rescue me from my fate. I was to be sent with other Austrian workers' children to the faraway country called the Netherlands to be fed and revitalized. . . .
>
> I was bundled up in whatever my parents could find and taken to the . . . Vienna railway station. There we waited long, tiring hours, during which we were joined by many other sickly children. Doctors looked me over, probing and examining my thin, weak, body. Although I was eleven, I looked much younger. . . . A card was hung around my neck. On it was printed a strange name, the name of people I had never met.[1]

Anne may not have known about Gies's childhood, but she did know that she could count on Gies in times of need or special danger. When Anne needed glasses, taking her to an oculist (an optometrist) became a major issue in the Secret Annexe:

> Sunday, 11 July 1943. . . . I'm so miserable and wretched as I've become very shortsighted and ought to have had glasses for a long time already (phew, what an owl I shall look!) but you know, of course, in hiding one cannot. Yesterday everyone talked of nothing but Anne's eyes, because Mummy had suggested sending me to the oculist with Mrs. Koophuis. I shook in my shoes somewhat at this announcement, for it is no small thing to do. Go out of doors, imagine it, in the street—doesn't

> bear thinking about! I was petrified at first, then glad. But it doesn't go as easily as that, because all the people who would have to approve such a step could not reach an agreement quickly. All the difficulties and risks had first to be carefully weighed, although Miep would have gone with me straight away. (Anne never did get her glasses; Mr. Frank decided that the risk was too great.)
>
> Miep . . . fetches and carries so much. Almost every day she manages to get hold of some vegetables for us and brings everything in shopping bags on her bicycle. We always long for Saturdays when our books come. Just like little children receiving a present.[2]

Punishment in Poland

Hiding Jews was dangerous anywhere, but in Poland, the penalty was especially severe. The Nazis also considered Poles inferior to Aryans, and the Nazi occupation forces treated them accordingly. Survivor David Landau explained: "Poles who were caught helping Jews in any way, be it only with a meal, were often shot without trial. If they were found hiding a Jew the most common punishment was the death of the whole family."[3]

On September 6, 1942, the SS and the police chief of Warsaw issued a proclamation:

> Re: Death Penalty for assistance to Jews who have left Jewish residential areas without permission.
>
> Numerous Jews have recently left the Jewish residential areas to which they were assigned. . . . They are still for the time being in the Warsaw district.
>
> I hereby declare that by the third decree of the Governor-General concerning residential restrictions . . . not only will Jews who in this way have left the

Expansion into Eastern Europe

In the early twentieth century, a school of thought arose that used Charles Darwin's theory of natural selection to theorize that in order to be successful and long-lasting, nations needed to adapt and expand. Many Germans were convinced that in order to be a strong country, Germany needed to grow, and they believed that Eastern Europe was the rightful home of the Germans. The Nazi Party planned to conquer countries across Eastern Europe, deport all Jews and other non-Aryan peoples, and adopt that space for the growing German empire. Poland, as the country immediately east of Germany, was the first nation that Hitler invaded in the quest for Germany to expand. The invasion of Poland in September 1939 is also the event that historians point to as the start of World War II.

residential areas assigned to them be punished with death but the same punishment will also be imposed on any person who knowingly harbours such Jews. This does not only include shelter and food but also any other sort of assistance, e.g. by conveying Jews in any sort of vehicles, by purchase of Jewish goods, etc.

I hereby instruct the population of the Warsaw District to inform the nearest police station or police command post immediately of any Jew who stays without authorisation outside a Jewish residential area.[4]

Child Protectors

The safety of hidden Jews and their protectors could rest on teenagers or even young children. One misspoken word or thoughtless action could spell doom for everyone involved. In spite of the danger, Heinrich Ebel, a German-born Pole with a seven-year-old daughter, agreed to shelter David Landau, his wife, and another couple:

> [Ebel] prepared a dug-out for us in the cellar as a hiding place to be used in moments of danger. In less threatening times, we could be hidden in his storeroom which adjoined his main living room. . . . [We had] the freedom of the house whenever possible. The four of us slept in one room together with [the Ebels'] seven-year-old daughter, who knew that we were the invisible people about whom nothing was to be spoken to anybody. She kept herself to this rule with absolute responsibility.
>
> When her mother asked her one evening, in our presence if she knew who the people in the room were, she turned with her face to us and asked her mother, "Which people, Mother?" When her mother pointed towards us the young girl once more asked in a very serious voice, "Do you feel well, Mother? There is nobody in the house except you, me and Father."[5]

Rachel Shtibel and the Olehreckys

Rachel Shtibel was only a bit older than the Ebels' daughter when Vasil and Maria Olehrecky sheltered her family. The Olehreckys once worked for Rachel's grandfather and had developed a close relationship with the family. Even when sheltering the Shtibels forced Vasil to volunteer for work in Germany, he refused to back down. In 1942, Rachel's

Heinrich Himmler, the chief of the SS, looks over a group of women and children in a destroyed village. Himmler was one of the most powerful men in Nazi Germany and is generally considered to be one of the primary engineers of the Holocaust.

parents learned that the Nazis were drafting young Polish men for work in Germany:

> Young men like Vasil. He knew that he could hide to escape the order, as others had done. But if he did, the Germans would come to search for him and they would find all of us. He decided that he would report voluntarily to the German authorities.
>
> The night before he left, Vasil came to say goodbye. "I told my wife to take care of you and I will write letters from Germany to see if you are alright."
>
> My father did not know what to say to this man who was putting himself in harm's way to help us. How to thank him. "I am sorry to have to put you through this. . . . You could hide. Maybe we should find another place." "No! You stay here. . . . You do not deserve a life like this. You are decent people and have always been good to my wife and me. If I can save you and you will all be alive when the war [is] over, this will be my reward." My father and Vasil hugged and cried together.
>
> That night was a very long one, and Vasil stayed with us in the barn until morning. My father tried to convince him not to go, that we could find another hiding place. But he would not hear of it. He knew that there was no place for us to go. . . . Vasil risked his marriage, his wife's life and his own life to save ours.[6]

Undercover for the Underground

When teenager Vladka Meed looked for a job on the Aryan side of Warsaw, she found both an employer and a loyal friend in Wanda Wnorowska:

> Wanda Wnorowska was one of the first Gentiles with whom I had any contact after I left the ghetto. The widow

Vladka Meed is pictured here in 1944 in Theater Square in the Aryan part of Warsaw, where she posed as a young Gentile woman and acted as a courier for the Jewish underground.

> of a Polish officer, she was in her forties and belonged to the so-called "better" Polish society. She operated a dressmaker's shop where I found employment almost as soon as I crossed to the "Aryan side." Not only was I assured of a job and warm quarters during the winter, but I also had an important front for my underground activities.
>
> When I was called upon to devote all my time to underground work and had to give up my job as a seamstress, Wanda gladly accepted in my place friends of mine who had just succeeded in getting out of the ghetto. She welcomed them all warmly and paid them relatively good wages. Wanda made friends with her new employees, took an interest in their difficulties, and endeavored not only to give them advice but also to help them through her contacts with other Gentiles.[7]

Dangers in the Household

Not everyone who sheltered Jews acted out of the kindness of their heart. Pani Karola worked as a housekeeper for a young priest. Anita Ekstein recognized that the housekeeper resented having to care for a child:

> She [Pani Karola] didn't know I was . . . Jewish. . . . I was supposed to be the niece of the priest. His sister had died and he agreed to bring me up. . . .
>
> Pani Karola was a terrible person. If she would have known that I was Jewish, my life wouldn't have been worth very much. Life, for me there was very hard, indeed. A priest is by no means rich and this was war time. Food was scarce. They had a small garden and they had a cow and I guess they existed on the produce from the garden and on the milk from the cow. . . .

> My task was to watch [the cow.] In Europe it was not like here [Canada] where you turn out the cows to pasture. There, if you had a cow, you had to have someone to watch it all day long. Wherever the cow went you went. . . . [This cow] got into all kinds of things. When I would stop and read a book and turn my head for a moment the cow would take off into the neighbour's patch and destroy their vegetables. Of course, I was punished for such things. One of the punishments was that I had to kneel on corn kernels for half an hour at a time.[8]

Bribes and Ransoms

Janina Bauman, whose Aunt Eugenia had predicted the Nazi atrocities, paid, along with her mother, and her sister, Sophie, for shelter in the home of an elderly couple who treated them more like guests than paid lodgers. Janina and Sophie called them Grannie and Grandad Sokolnicki. Janina described them as "warm, understanding people, of deep culture . . . and tact."[9]

The Sokolnickis' widowed daughter ran the household. She was brisk and matter-of-fact, known to Janina and her family only as Mrs. Serbin. She ran a tight household, especially where food was concerned:

> From the very first evening I knew we would not starve any more, but at the same time I suspected we would not get enough to feel comfortable either. This was right. The portions of tasty, nicely arranged food we received would not have fed a baby. Grannie and Klara [Mrs. Serbin's sister] were both well aware of this and always looked away embarrassed when they brought our meals. It wasn't their fault—we knew very

Members of the Gestapo, pictured in their uniforms, confiscate material from a Jewish home in Poland in July 1941.

> well that they would have gladly served us [more] if it had been up to them. They were in Mrs. Serbin's hands, however—she kept the larder [pantry] locked and the key in her pocket after she had given out the daily ration of food in the morning.[10]

The family's safety ended abruptly when the Warsaw ghetto went up in flames after the uprising of 1943. The Nazis looked for survivors all over the city. Janina remembered the night they came to the Sokolnickis' house:

> In my sleep I heard violent knocking at the door and woke up in terror. In the faint light of the dawn I saw Mrs. Serbin. Three tall men in dark hats and black leather jackets pushed by her, making their way into our room. "Your documents, Mrs. Lubowicki," shouted Mrs. Serbin, "the gentlemen wish to see your *Kennkarten*." . . . Her hands trembling, Mother quickly produced the three identification cards that she always kept by her bed in her handbag. One of the men turned the light on, but did not look at the documents: he stared straight at Mother's terrified face while his companions [looked at] Sophie and me. "Jewish," they concluded. "Get up at once, you are coming with us," said the first man icily. He spoke Polish.
>
> They gave us five minutes to get ready and left the room, taking Mrs. Serbin with them. After a while she was back, her face flaming, her voice breaking. "Money," she panted. "They are willing to leave you alone if you pay them. Mrs. Lubowicki, you must do it . . . for the sake of all of us."[11]

The Nazis agreed to an amount and arranged to pick up the money in three days:

> There was no time to waste: our shelter had ceased to be safe, for our own and our hosts' sake we had to leave at once. . . . If only we could get out of the way, [a family friend] could somehow raise the money for the ransom and Mrs. Serbin would be able to cope with the rascals more easily alone.[12]

Janina and her family ran from the Sokolnickis' house and began a desperate search for another safe haven.

The Candle Factory

Because the Nazis would not allow Jews to own businesses, Nechama Tec's father transferred ownership of his candle factory to a longtime employee, Mr. Pys:

> He had also left Mr. Pys many valuable household items, including crystal, silver, and expensive china. Grateful for what he had received, and also for the trust my parents had in him, Mr. Pys had agreed to our taking refuge in his home if events forced us to leave the factory. The time had come to take advantage of his offer—a generous one indeed, for by taking us in he would put himself and his family in jeopardy. . . . Of the four of us, my mother went first, accompanied to the Pys apartment by a trustworthy Polish factory worker. She was dressed, as planned, as a Polish lady in mourning. No one recognized her, and no one would have taken her for a runaway Jew. My sister went next, going with another worker we trusted. My father and I left together, a few minutes after my sister.
>
> Even though the arrangements had been made in advance, the Pys family was not overjoyed by our arrival. Mrs. Pys's mother, who lived with them, had been born a Jew and had converted to Catholicism as

> a little girl. The family was fearful that if the Germans discovered her origins that alone would place them in real danger—and our presence put them in double jeopardy. They made it plain that they regretted their offer of help.
>
> Father tried to calm them by assuring them that we had no intention of staying long. Indeed . . . we were already in close touch with the young Pole who had come to lead us out of Lublin. But for the time being it was best to stay in the house.[13]

In spite of their fear, the Pys family risked everything to help their Jewish friends. Like Miep Gies, Heinrich Ebel, and others, they put themselves in danger to help people survive.

Chapter 5

Polish Ghettos and the Rise of the Resistance

In January 1942, a group of Nazi leaders held a meeting to work out the details of the "final solution": a plan to murder all the Jews of Europe in order to create a massive German ethnostate across the continent.. The killing itself had already begun, in ghettos and labor camps and death camps, but the killing became even more widespread when Germany invaded the Soviet Union in June 1941. German killing squads called Einsatzgruppen followed the regular army, and after the army had occupied a town or village, it was the Einsatzgruppen's job to round up all the Jews that were left and kill them, usually by shooting them.

At the same time, the Nazis began deporting Jews from ghettos in Poland and other occupied countries. Early on in the Holocaust, poor neighborhoods in different cities were cleared out, and Jews were forced to relocate to these areas, called ghettos. The ghettos were slowly isolated more and more from the rest of the city, and often people living in ghettos had minimal access to food and other necessities, like medical care. People could be shot at any

Women and children in a line prepare to be deported to death camps in Eastern Europe. Early on in the liquidation process, most didn't realize that they were headed to their deaths. The Star of David, which Jews were forced to wear, can easily be seen on some of the women's coats.

The Wannsee Conference

"The final solution" was the euphemistic term for the genocide of Europe's Jews in order to make room for the new Aryan German state. It's not clear when Nazi leaders decided that the final solution was the best course of action, but historians pinpoint the Wannsee Conference as the meeting during which the final solution was set in motion. At some point in 1941, Hitler authorized mass murder of the Jewish people in Europe. In January 1942, fifteen members of the Nazi Party and the Nazi-led German government met in Wannsee, a suburb of Berlin, to discuss the systematic implementation of the final solution. Although many thousands of Jews had already been murdered, this meeting represented the start of a coordinated effort on behalf of the government, the Nazi Party, and all affiliated military groups to begin the eradication of all Jews in Europe.

time while living in the ghettos, but eventually the ghettos were "liquidated," meaning that they were emptied and everyone was killed. Jews were sent by the trainload from ghettos to death camps, where the majority of new arrivals at these camps went straight to the gas chambers.

The Bunker and the Farmhouse

As the ghettos were liquidated, many people found that forests and farms offered safer hiding places than the perilous, Nazi-ridden ghettos. In the winter of 1943, Nazi soldiers roamed the streets of a ghetto in eastern Poland, prepared to shoot any Jews they came across. Panic spread throughout the ghetto: many people screaming, running, trying to hide. Fifteen-year-old Fela Steinberg was with her mother at the time. The two of them stumbled upon a bunker and crawled in to hide. Above them and from all directions, rifle fire cracked through the winter air. Fela and her mother huddled together, both of them silent and shivering in the cold. The rest of their family was trapped in the dying ghetto.

Fela's father had planned for this moment, hiding money and valuables with Polish friends and building two hiding places: an emergency bunker in town and a larger one in the forest. One day, out of nowhere, the Nazis added a small quantity of meat to the ghetto rations, which alarmed Mr. Steinberg. He encouraged his family to hide, but Fela's sister resisted. The family decided to wait, not knowing it was already too late.

Many years later, Fela Steinberg explained what happened after that:

> At four o'clock in the morning the shooting started. We were caught off-guard. When my father said, "Children, this is it," I panicked and ran out. I did not know where. . . . Outside I saw my mother running, and she grabbed my hand. She was going in the direction of the guards and the ghetto wire. I tried to pull her away from there, and she started to scream that she wanted to go back to father. I could see from the outside that they were already in our house. I pulled my mother with me and we followed the crowd.[1]

Fela and her mother raced away from the gunfire and jumped into a trench. It led to a small bunker, which seemed to be empty at the time. They huddled together, waiting until long after the shooting stopped. When they crawled out into the sunlight, they discovered that they had not been alone in the bunker. A young man named Romek had shared the space. Fela and her mother knew him from the ghetto, and so the three of them set off in search of a new place to hide.

They went into the countryside and visited one farmhouse after another. Each time, Fela would knock on the door and ask for shelter, and each time, she was turned away. At nightfall, they finally found a place. A peasant couple known only as Stach and Magda agreed to shelter Fela, but Romek and Mrs. Steinberg would have to leave in the morning. They looked "too Jewish," Magda said. Someone in the area would surely report them to the Nazis and then everyone would suffer.

Fela did not care about the risks. If her mother had to leave in the morning, then she would go with her. Everyone was too tired to argue the matter, so Magda spread some straw on the barn floor and the three runaways lay down to sleep. When Fela woke in the morning, her mother was gone; she had slipped away before daylight and taken Romek with her.

Mrs. Steinberg's Sacrifice

Mrs. Steinberg left word with Magda that she would be back as soon as she found a suitable hiding place. Fela stayed with Stach and Magda, but guilt gnawed at her day and night. She had a safe home with people who treated her well. Her mother was out there somewhere, maybe lost, freezing, or maybe dead or dying. When Fela could no longer bear the uncertainty, she set out to find her mother.

After a long and fruitless search, Fela finally accepted the hard truth: she would never see her mother again. She did see Romek one more time. He returned to Stach and Magda's to explain what had happened.

Mrs. Steinberg never found a permanent hiding place. She bounced from one place to another, growing more and more tired and dispirited with every move. She never stopped mourning the family she had lost and never stopped blaming herself for leaving them behind in the ghetto. When the burden became unbearable, Mrs. Steinberg simply quit. She stopped looking for hiding places and became resigned to a miserable fate. One day she saw a group of Jews being led away by Nazis. Without hesitation, she joined their march and became another victim of the Holocaust.

Fela mourned her mother not only because she died, but also because she died alone, without hope or comfort. This was the way of life in Nazi-occupied Poland.

Though Fela had to leave Stach and Magda when the neighbors started asking too many questions, she managed to survive. She went from one hiding place to another until a kindly priest gave her a Christian birth certificate. Armed with that, Fela no longer had to move from one hiding place to another. She found safe hiding that lasted for the rest of the war. After the fighting had ended, Fela learned that her father, sister, and three brothers had perished in the ghetto. None of them made it to the bunkers her father had worked so hard to build.

Prisoners march to Dachau, the first of the concentration camps established in Germany. This photo was taken without the Nazis' knowledge by Maria Seidenberger as her mother stood outside.

Joining the Resistance

When Jews came to realize what was happening in the ghettos, some young people decided to fight back. They hid in bunkers and secret apartments; they fled the ghettos and work camps to hide in the forests of Europe. With nothing left to lose, they prepared to resist the enemy. They did not expect to conquer a huge force with superior weapons. They expected only to go down fighting and make the Germans pay dearly for every victory.

The difficult process that would turn teenager Simha Rotem into a resistance fighter codenamed "Kazik" began soon after the Germans occupied Warsaw in 1939. Because of his appearance and upbringing, Simha was not easily identified as a Jew. He had blond hair, blue eyes, and was comfortable with both the Polish language and culture.

Before the Nazis sealed the ghetto, he would go into nearby villages to buy food:

> The illegal trade in food began to flourish right after the Germans introduced rationing. Basic foods became rarities, but you could usually still get them for a

high price in the villages. If you managed to smuggle your wares (sausages, potatoes, eggs, cheese) into the city, you could make a lot of money. I decided to do something to provide food for my family; I went to the villages several times and brought home enough food

Members of the Jewish resistance in Poland hold their arms up after being captured by Nazi soldiers during the Warsaw ghetto rebellion. Nazi soldiers can be seen in the background.

> to last a few weeks. If you were lucky on the train or the road—and if the Germans didn't search your bags—you succeeded. If you weren't lucky and got caught, the food was confiscated and you got beaten. Even at this stage, in trips to the villages, I looked like a Polish Christian. I was fifteen years old and looked just like a Gentile.[2]

Looking "just like a Gentile" helped Simha and his family survive in the early days. However, after the Nazis sealed the ghetto, people dropped dead of starvation in the streets:

> Hungry people wandered around the Ghetto. Rations were substandard. You couldn't live on them, and those who had to make do with them were doomed to a slow death. Contagious diseases soon began spreading in the Ghetto, especially typhus. People swollen with hunger were seen in the [streets], rummaging through garbage cans and searching for scraps of food. Corpses were scattered about before being picked up in wheelbarrows going through the Ghetto and taken to the cemetery. These sights became routine; we started getting used to them and even grew indifferent.
>
> To escape from hunger, my family started doing what others did: selling everything we had on the flourishing black market. Gangs of smugglers, especially youths, went into that business. . . . They banded together with groups outside the Ghetto, who threw them food over the wall. The Germans would open fire whenever they came on the smugglers, but hunger was oppressive and people took risks.
>
> I tried my hand at smuggling a few times. My parents opposed it for fear I would get hurt, but when hunger intensified at home, no one could stop me. Apparently I was rather successful. Friends and relatives used to

> come to us for a bowl of soup, a sign that there was at least some food in our house.[3]

With his forged identity papers, Simha moved to the Aryan side of Warsaw and joined the underground. He became a courier, shuttling supplies, money, and information between the Aryan side of Warsaw and the safehouses and hidden bunkers of the ghetto. After the ghetto uprising of April 19 to May 16, 1943, Simha helped to rescue survivors from the smoldering ruins and get them into safe hiding:

> I took on various missions and errands. We couriers tried to carry out these missions without an escort, and only rarely . . . was I accompanied by anyone. Our tasks were:
>
> 1. maintaining contact with people in the camps and ghettos; preserving this contact between them and free Jews—who were in touch with the Polish underground and knew what was going on in the world and on the front—was important and encouraging.
> 2. delivering money and financial assistance to various branches of the organization.
> 3. delivering forged documents.
> 4. delivering underground publications.
> 5. supplying weapons to places where uprisings were planned and prepared.[4]

Digging Toward Safety

In Staszow, Poland, Maurice Frydman heard that the Nazis were resettling Jews someplace east. At the time, Maurice and his comrades did not know that resettled Jews went straight to death camps. They did know that survival depended on escaping Nazi control:

> We decided to build a shelter in the forest. To have there a place to stay, to have familiar people around who could give us food and whatever. There were 12 or 15 people who built that shelter. It was underground, masked so nobody really could see it. If you wanted you could cover the entrance. There was a bush growing there, I remember the bush. We could stay there until the danger passed. It was in a . . . forest, so it was very unlikely that people would walk around for no reason. That worked quite well for a while.
>
> We got a message about 8 days before the "resettlement" [order] came to Staszow. It was to take place on a certain day. . . . so we took to that shelter in the forest [outside of Staszow]. Then, a couple days later, we heard that yes, the order came, they took all the Jews out, they took them to a railroad station and carried them away. There was a Jewish labor camp left in town. . . . That provided some degree of safety. We didn't believe it, so we decided not to [go there].[5]

Maurice's group literally dug into their hiding place:

> We dug a hole, maybe 12'x 12', 6' or 8' high, put a wooden structure made of plywood in it, put about 12 inches of soil on top of it, planted some plants in it. There was an entrance, maybe two and a half feet by two and a half feet, which could be opened from the inside. A ventilation channel was placed between 3 bushes so it wouldn't be seen. It was erected scientifically. We could stay there a couple of days, or longer, especially when it snowed. You don't want to have any tracks around it. With 15 people it was very crowded, though not all 15 were in there all [at] one time. Some stayed out.

> You could cook, but only at night not in the day-time, because the smell of fire could lead people to it. . . . You don't want to leave any traces of your presence.[6]

Hiding from Death

Gertrude Wechsler Jorisch was in a work camp when rumors of mass exterminations began circulating:

> [We] heard . . . that the [Germans were] going to liquidate the camp and kill everybody, and make the town completely free of Jews. A group of teenagers in which I was included . . . decided [to] . . . try to escape from camp to the forest. . . . It was in the middle of the night, we started on our journey . . . it was scary. We did not think we would make it, but there was no other way. We had to take the chance. It was live or die.
>
> The Germans with their dogs . . . were all over guarding the camp. The hardest thing was to sneak through the barbed wires and the swamps. We did it. Walking through the swamps my father's foot got stuck in the mud. My [boyfriend] Martin pulled him out of the mud put him on his shoulders and carried my father through the swamps and the lake. It was unbelievable.
>
> Once we were on the other side of the lake we felt a little safer. . . . Tired, exhausted and beat we finally reached the forest of Ostra Mogila thinking this is our last chance to survive or die like animals. . . . For the next 13 months we lived in the forest, this was our home, we found a bunker and slept in it, during the day we [went] running through the forest. It was [too] dangerous to stay in one place. . . . the Ukrainians and the Poles found out that the Jews [were] using the water from the water well and they came and threw rocks, mud and garbage into the well. . . . that was the end of the water, we had to rely on rain or snow.

Not Just Nazis

It was not unusual for Jewish forest dwellers to hide from Ukrainians and Poles as well as Nazis. Many Ukrainians and Poles were anti-Semitic and would not put their hatred aside, even to fight Nazis. In June 1943, Maurice Frydman's group had to leave their forest hideaway because of the different varieties of the Polish underground.

> Some of them were helping Jews. Some of them were killing Jews. The "bad" guys were walking around trying to find the hiding places. My mother got killed that way. [She] went out . . . and was approached by these Polish underground [members] and got killed right on the spot.
>
> So it was too dangerous to stay in one place, too dangerous to stay in the forest. We managed to get shelter in a little village called Czajkow. There were several people there. They built a shelter in a barn on a farm. . . . The Germans came and inspected [the] farm, but they found nothing. . . . We stayed there until August . . . of '44 when the Russians came in [and liberated the area].[8]

> Life without water became unbearable, we could not wash ourselves we became infected with lice, they were multiplying by the thousands. . . . We had to think about food . . . so we decided to go at night to the field and [steal] potatoes. [We used] to make a fire only at night [to] bake them and eat them. Potatoes were the only thing we could get. We looked like skeletons, our intestines were so dried that we could not even digest the potatoes.[7]

Survival in the Ruins

By October 1944, most Germans realized that the war was hopeless. In a matter of months, they would surrender to the Allies (Great Britain, the United States, and the Soviet Union), ending the war in Europe. In these last weeks and months, they destroyed as much as they could: waterworks, electric plants, bridges, even whole towns and cities.

As the Nazis laid waste to Warsaw, David Landau and other surviving Jews clung to life in underground bunkers:

> The word "eerie" in English could have been invented for the empty . . . ruins of Warsaw after its remaining inhabitants had been removed.
>
> During daytime the surface of Warsaw was inhabited by dogs; the Germans . . . emptied the buildings of anything valuable and [burned] them. Berlin had [ordered] that Warsaw was to be erased from the map of Europe before the Germans left. . . .
>
> [Beneath the ruined city], Jews [lived in] caverns and bunkers, like moles. . . . In the daytime the underground inhabitants lay hidden while the [Germans] did their [work]. During the hours of darkness, the Germans removed themselves from the streets to stay behind the closed gates of some buildings. Inside their temporary

Members of the Polish underground plan to create a diversion in Pogorzne, Poland.

> fortresses they made small fires by which they kept themselves warm during the winter nights. In those dark hours the moles surfaced. They roamed the same streets and buildings seeking food, clothing, shoes and sometimes [fuel] to illuminate their hiding places.[9]

The Taste of Freedom

When the war finally ended and the Germans fled, surviving resistance fighters began coming out of hiding. David Landau and his companions in the bunker were so used to danger that they did not believe the first news they heard:

> Halfway through January we began to hear heavy artillery and bombing. We hoped to hear details of the action [on the radio] but just at this critical time [the station] went off the air. . . . On 17 January we heard Russian songs outside. . . . [later] Somebody began knocking on our secret entrance desperately telling us that we should come out, the Germans had fled. Of course, we knew that it was a German trick. . . . The caller kept on for some time but finally left. . . . nobody went to sleep that night. In the morning the same voice came back. Knocking on the entrance: "The Russians are here! We are free!" As we did not answer, the caller seemed to become fed up: "I'll not come back again to call you if you don't believe me. But before I go, open and let me slide in. Have your revolvers ready. If the Germans follow me you may shoot me first, I'll slide head in first, just open the entrance."
>
> We risked it and the man slid inwards. . . . He had brought us a page of a proclamation in Polish and in Russian as evidence. We were indeed free.[10]

For the surviving resistance fighters, freedom was only the beginning. They had to rebuild shattered lives, and find hope and meaning for the future. Many became activists: working for a Jewish homeland in Palestine, exposing many Nazi war criminals, pressing for human rights, and advocating for laws to help protect society from hate mongers like Adolf Hitler.

No matter what they accomplished, the surviving freedom fighters could never forget the horror, the suffering, and the dying. It was part of their life experience, but so was the courage that made them fight a battle that everyone knew they could not win.

Chapter 6

Rebuilding and Devastation at the End of the War

On May 8, 1945, Germany surrendered unconditionally to the Allied forces, but the end of the war did not mean the end of of suffering or Jews' persecution. Stunned soldiers reported liberating camps filled with dead and dying Jews whom they were too late to save. They saw mass graves, piles of ashes from crematory ovens, and corpses lying uncovered on the ground.

The death and destruction was impossible to fully comprehend: it is thought that nearly six million Jews died in the Holocaust, and millions of others, including Romani, disabled people, political dissidents, and social outcasts were killed as well. Nazi Germany had expanded Hitler's reach beyond German borders into Austria, Poland, and parts of Norway and France, and there was an incalculable amount of societal rebuilding left to do. As governments and communities sought to recover, individual survivors struggled to adjust to freedom and take back their lives.

After the liberation of Auschwitz, a doctor (*center*) stands with prisoners outside the concentration camp. Soviet soldiers in the Red Army liberated the camp on January 27, 1945.

Riding Toward Home

When the war ended, Yehuda Nir, along with his mother and sister, set out for Warsaw and whatever might be left of their home:

> So it was time again for packing. God knows how many times we had done it since that fateful autumn of 1939. Each time there had been less to pack, our belongings dwindling and their importance becoming secondary to survival. . . . I was in a hurry to get out of there, to return to circumstances that would at least have [the appearance] of normality. . . . we took a [cart] with the only horse left in the stable. . . . I was riding behind the cart on my bike . . . absorbed in my thoughts, full of conflicting emotions. I was thinking of all the people who probably hadn't survived the war: Father; my little cousin Juleczek . . . my aunts and uncles; my many cousins. I hoped that some of them had been as lucky as we. I also thought of how I would be going back to school. I wouldn't have to lie and pretend anymore. Soon we might be able to join our family in Palestine . . . Jabotinsky Street, Tel Aviv [present-day Israel].[1]

Converting Back to Judaism

Many survivors dreamed of going home, only to realize that the world they left behind no longer existed. They had no place to go and no family left to care about them. Some hidden children had passed as Christians for so long that they did not want to reclaim their Jewish identities. Anita Ekstein loved her foster parents and wanted to stay with them:

> I was told that . . . no one was left from my family. In order to stay with the Matusiewicz family and be part of

> them, I would have to become a Catholic. I really didn't mind it by then. . . . I believed everything I was taught in the bible classes and I wanted to become a Catholic and be part of them and their family. Therefore, in June, 1945, I was baptized. I was given first communion and I became a full-fledged Catholic. I had accepted the fact that my entire family was dead and that I would live and grow up with the Matusiewicz family.[2]

Several months later, Anita discovered that her aunt Sala Stern had survived and wanted to take her to live in the nearby town of Katowice, where Stern had a home. She also wanted Anita to renounce Catholicism and reclaim her Jewish heritage:

> She couldn't bear the thought that I was a Catholic and . . . wanted me to change immediately . . . of course, I couldn't. I needed time to think . . . and to take it all in.
>
> Every time we went out and passed a church I'd run in, get down on my knees and pray. She would come and drag me out. . . . I was afraid of Jews, I really was. I had been taught . . . that Jews were not good. . . . That they were evil people.

Stern eventually brought Anita to Paris, where they lived for two years. During that time, Anita became accustomed to living among Jews. She began to slowly regain her Jewish identity: "I began to realize that I had to be proud that I was Jewish and I had to remain Jewish for my parents' sake. In time, I stopped going to church."[3] Anita eventually married a Jewish man and raised their three children as Jews.

Dual Identities

Like Anita Ekstein, many young Jews had trouble reconciling their Jewish and Aryan identities. Others came to terms with themselves because of a meaningful encounter with their own Jewishness.

Magda Denes belonged to the latter group. Her defining moment came in the waning days of the war, when the Germans staggered under near-constant aerial bombardment:

> Air raid sirens woke me. Through the double-shuttered windows, they sounded faint, ghosts whistling an eerie dirge in the dark. . . . The explosions started before the third round of warning was over. Antiaircraft guns responded in furious staccato. I wasn't very frightened until later, when I heard the detonations come nearer and nearer. . . . An astonishing realization struck. I knew only the first two words of the Jewish prayer for a time of danger and dying: *Shema Yisrael.* I could not die all alone, without even God for company. I would have to do what I had learned not long ago: kneel and say their prayer. "Our Father who art in heaven." It didn't seem right. . . . [to] address god in Christian in the hour of my Jewish death. I thought I should learn *Shema Yisrael* in its entirety. Fast.[4]

The Boy in the Shed

After the war ended, Jews came out of hiding, and Germans who had served in the occupational army or worked in the camps also suddenly needed places of refuge. This was especially true in Poland, where the Germans had slaughtered Jews by the tens of thousands and treated gentile Poles as less than human.

Janina Bauman took this hatred of Germans for granted until her Polish rescuer sent her on a strange errand:

> For us the war came to an . . . end at 8 A.M. on Friday, 19 January 1945. After a sleepless night echoing with cannon-fire, heavy with great expectations, we saw in the faint light of the wintry dawn the . . . hunched outlines of the first Russian soldiers. . . . [They] scuttled, one by one past our window, their guns at the ready. By noon the sounds of heavy battle subsided and were replaced by a steady rumble of heavy vehicles coming from afar.
>
> Just before dusk I went out to fetch some wood. In the semidark shed, crammed with logs and tools, something stirred. I sensed a human presence. I pushed the door wide open to let in more light. Only then did I notice a flap of field-grey military coat sticking out from between two logs. Calmly, I locked the shed and ran back to the cottage. In the kitchen, Mrs. Pietrzyk . . . was busy cooking. Gasping for breath, I told her what I had seen. But she was not surprised: she already knew. Staring full in my face with her ancient, all-knowing eyes, she said, . . . "Whoever comes under my roof seeking shelter, no matter who he is, no matter what he believes in, he will be safe with me." In a flash I understood. . . . I watched her fill a . . . bowl with hot dumplings and pour pork fat over it. "Hold it, child," she [said]. "Take it to him." . . . I blindly obeyed and went back to the shed. It seemed as deserted as before, even the field-grey flap had disappeared. I stood [with] the hot dish burning my fingers and filling the air with a strong smell of food. There was a brief commotion behind the pile of logs and an unkempt head suddenly popped out. I saw the pale face of the German, a boy rather than a man,

Warsaw residents shop in an outdoor market in the middle of the bombed out city. Warsaw, the Polish capital, suffered heavy bombing during World War II.

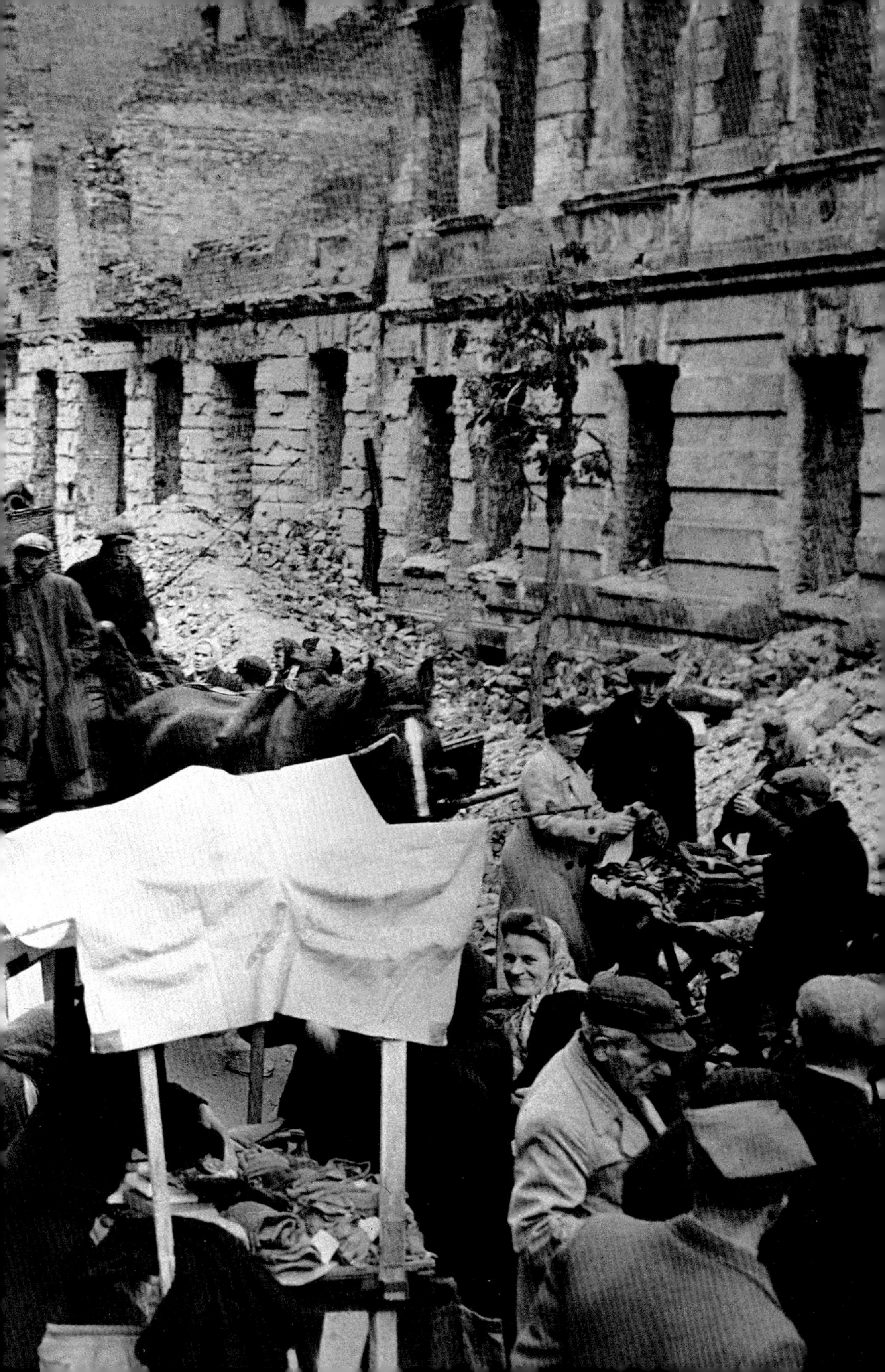

> staring at me in terror. He grabbed the steaming bowl from my hands and fell on the food with unspeakable greed. He was still trembling from hunger and fear. For a long while, I watched him blankly. I felt no pity, no hatred, no joy.[5]

Finding a Way to Rebuild

Every young survivor paid a price for his or her life: grief, unwanted memories, nightmares that would never go away. When the war ended, those who had lived in secret

Lasting Effects

After experiencing a traumatic event or series of events, many people experience symptoms of a condition called post-traumatic stress disorder (PTSD). These symptoms often include depression, sudden bursts of fear or rage, flashbacks either during the day or while dreaming, avoidance of things that might remind them of the traumatic experience, and memory issues like amnesia surrounding the event.[6] Doctors were diagnosing people with PTSD as early as World War I, though back then it was called shell shock, and it was treated very differently.[7] Readjusting to life after the Holocaust meant dealing with many of these symptoms at a time when few people truly understood the issue or how to treat it. Survivors often reported having holes in their memories, reliving memories in nightmares, and other difficult psychological experiences that are in fact normal reactions to experiencing major trauma, especially at such a young age.

hiding places had to return to a normal life. Those who lived under false identities had to come to terms with their true identity.

For Ezra BenGershôm, the road to freedom in Israel began in the shadow of the past:

> The train bore me away from the capital of Hitler's Germany towards saving frontiers. I recall my successful escape—yet I do so without joy. A glance at the map shows that the first half of my journey coincided with the route from Berlin to Auschwitz [a concentration camp and, later, death camp in Poland]. On the very rails that bore me to safety, unnumbered thousands were freighted punctually to their deaths. The [same] inspectors and crossing keepers did duty for both sorts of traffic as far as that point . . . where the line branched off to the biggest of the German death camps. . . . The managers of the state railway company knew. Hitler could count on them. And who could doubt the utter reliability of the lesser officials . . . the stationmasters, the drivers, the pointsmen? I have not heard of a single instance of a train bound for Auschwitz being accidentally switched to Vienna. My train turned south. The smoke clouds of the crematoria were well out of visual range. In any case, I had long since been rocked to sleep by the rumble of the wheels.[8]

Like survivors of any age, children and teens could not escape the past, nor forget the Holocaust. By moving on in spite of the memories and the pain, they not only reclaimed their lives, but also honored the memories of the six million Jews who perished.

Timeline

1939

September 1—Germany invades Poland.

1940

February 8—Establishment of the Lodz ghetto.

April 9—Germany invades Denmark and Norway.

April 30—Lodz ghetto sealed off; Jews not allowed to go outside its boundaries.

May 10—Germany invades Holland, Belgium, and France.

October 16—Warsaw ghetto established.

November 16—Warsaw ghetto sealed off; Jews not allowed to leave.

1941

June 22—Germany invades Soviet Union; *Einsatzgruppen* death squads begin slaughter of Jews.

July 31—SS officer Reinhard Heydrich is ordered to "solve the Jewish problem by means of emigration and evacuation."

October 23—Jews forbidden to emigrate from the German Reich (Empire).

1942

January 20—Wannsee conference prepares to coordinate the "final solution" to the Jewish question.

March—Belzec annihilation camp becomes operational.

March 17–24—Massive deportations of Jews to Belzec, Auschwitz, and other camps. With each round of deportations, more Jews go into hiding.

1943

April 19–May 16—Warsaw ghetto uprising; Jewish survivors hide in bunkers or escape to the forest.

June 21—SS orders complete destruction of all ghettos in Poland.

1944

March 19—Germany invades Hungary.

1945

January—Allies advance on German positions; camp guards begin forced marches of Jewish prisoners.

January 17—Soviet troops liberate Warsaw.

January 27 —Soviet troops liberate Auschwitz, and Jews begin to come out of hiding as other camps and towns are liberated.

April 30—Adolf Hitler commits suicide.

May 8—Germany surrenders unconditionally to the Allies.

Chapter Notes

Introduction

1. Adolf Hitler, *Hitler's Table Talk, 1941–1944: His Private Conversations*, translated by Norman Cameron and H.R. Stevens (New York: Enigma Books, 2007), p. 87.

Chapter 1

To Leave or to Stay?

1. *Das Schwarze Korps*, Munich: Franz Eber Verlag, November 24, 1938, translation in Benno Müller-Hill, *Murderous Science* (New York, NY: CSHL Press, 1998), p. 44.
2. Janina Bauman, *Winter in the Morning: A Young Girl's Life in the Warsaw Ghetto and Beyond 1939–1945* (New York, NY: The Free Press, 1986), p. 7.
3. Norman Feld, USHMM Archives, ACC 1991.066.02.056.
4. Ibid.
5. Ezra BenGershôm, *David: Testimony of a Holocaust Survivor* (Oxford, England: Oswald Wolff Books, 1988), p. 152.
6. Ibid., pp. 152–153.
7. Ibid., p. 177.
8. Ibid., p. 187.
9. Brenda Szyr Senders, USHMM Interview, RG-50.030*0212.
10. Olga Sher with Margrit Rosenberg Stenge, *Olga's Story* (The Concordia University Chair in Canadian Jewish Studies and The Montreal Institute for Genocide and Human Rights Studies, 2002).
11. Sally Eisner, "Personal Reflections—In Hiding," 2005, http://fcit.usf.edu/holocaust/people/survivor.htm.

Chapter 2

Safe Spaces and Secret Places

1. Anne Frank, *Anne Frank: The Diary of a Young Girl* (Garden City, NY: Doubleday, 1967), p. 23.
2. Ibid., p. 25.
3. Ibid., p. 26.
4. Ibid., pp. 27–29.
5. Ibid., p. 32.

6. Rachel Shtibel, *The Violin*, The Concordia University Chair in Canadian Jewish Studies, 2002, http://migs.concordia.ca/memoirs/shtibel/rachel_shtibel_02.htm.
7. Bronia Beker, "In Hiding," Women and the Holocaust: Personal Reflections, 2001, https://www.fold3.com/page/285875802_holocaust_survivors_their_stories/stories.
8. Ibid.
9. Aaron Elster Memoir, USHMM Archives 1998.A.0017.
10. Ibid.
11. Norman Feld, USHMM Archives, ACC 1991.066.02.056.
12. Frank, pp. 290–292.

Chapter 3

In Plain Sight

1. Judy Cohen, "Personal Reflections—In Hiding: Anita Ekstein," 2001, http://www3.sympatico.ca/mighty1/personal/anita.htm.
2. Ibid.
3. Magda Lipner, USHMM Survivor Testimonies, RG-02.205.
4. Anita Magnus Frank, USHMM Survivor Testimonies, RG-50.030*0072.
5. Ibid.
6. Ibid.
7. Raszka (Roza) Galek, "Personal Histories: Children," USHMM, n.d., https://www.ushmm.org/exhibition/personal-history/media_oi.php?MediaId=1196.
8. Lipner.
9. Ibid.
10. Stacy Cretzmeyer, *Your Name Is Renee: Ruth Kapp Hartz's Story as a Hidden Child in Nazi-Occupied France* (New York, NY: Oxford University Press, 1994), pp. 14–15.
11. Barbara Ledermann Rodbell, "Personal Histories: Children," USHMM, n.d., https://www.ushmm.org/exhibition/personal-history/media_oi.php?MediaId=2846&th=children.
12. Yehuda Nir, *The Lost Childhood: A Memoir* (New York, NY: Harcourt Brace Jovanovich, 2002), p. 56.
13. Ibid., pp. 56–57.
14. Ibid., p. 60.
15. Ibid., p. 63.
16. Ibid. pp. 48–49.
17. Ibid., pp. 122–125.

18. Leah Hammerstein Silverstein, "Personal Histories: Children," USHMM, n.d., https://www.ushmm.org/exhibition/personal history/media_oi.php?MediaId=1181&th=children).
19. David J. Landau, *Caged: The Landau Manuscript* (self-published, 1999), pp. 253–254.

Chapter 4

Protectors and Persecution

1. Miep Gies and Alison Leslie Gold, *Anne Frank Remembered* (New York, NY: Simon & Schuster, 1988), pp. 17–18.
2. Anne Frank, *Anne Frank: The Diary of a Young Girl* (Garden City, NY: Doubleday, 1967), p. 98.
3. David J. Landau, *Caged: The Landau Manuscript* (self-published, 1999), p. 251.
4. Janina Bauman, *Winter in the Morning: A Young Girl's Life in the Warsaw Ghetto and Beyond 1939–1945* (New York, NY: The Free Press, 1986), p. 98.
5. Landau, p. 250.
6. Rachel Shtibel, *The Violin*, The Concordia University Chair in Canadian Jewish Studies, 2002, http://migs.concordia.ca/memoirs/shtibel/rachel_shtibel_02.htm.
7. Vladka Meed, *On Both Sides of the Wall: Memoirs From the Warsaw Ghetto* (Washington, DC: United States Holocaust Memorial Museum Edition, 1993), p. 190.
8. Judy Cohen, "Personal Reflections—In Hiding: Anita Ekstein," 2001, http://www3.sympatico.ca/mighty1/personal/anita.htm.
9. Bauman, p. 101.
10. Ibid., pp. 103–104.
11. Ibid., p. 111.
12. Ibid., p. 112.
13. Nechama Tec, *Dry Tears: The Story of a Lost Childhood* (New York, NY: Oxford University Press, 1984), pp. 38–39.

Chapter 5

Polish Ghettos and the Rise of the Resistance

1. Nechama Tec, *When Light Pierced the Darkness: Christian Rescue of Jews in Nazi-Occupied Poland* (New York, NY: Oxford University Press, 1986), p. 43.
2. Kazik (Simha Rotem), *Memoirs of a Warsaw Ghetto Fighter* (Danbury, CT: Yale University Press, 1994), p. 11.
3. Ibid., pp. 12–13.

4. Ibid., p. 67.
5. Maurice Frydman, Oral History Interview, USHMM Archives 2006.78.
6. Ibid.
7. Gertrude Wechsler Jorisch, Memoir, USHMM Archives 2007.75.
8. Frydman.
9. David J. Landau, *Caged: The Landau Manuscript* (self-published, 1999), p. 281.
10. Ibid., p. 286.

Chapter 6

Rebuilding and Devastation at the End of the War

1. Yehuda Nir, *The Lost Childhood: A Memoir* (New York, NY: Harcourt Brace Jovanovich, 2002), pp. 264–266.
2. Judy Cohen, "Personal Reflections—In Hiding: Anita Ekstein," 2001, http://www3.sympatico.ca/mighty1/personal/anita.htm.
3. Ibid.
4. Magda Denes, *Castles Burning: A Child's Life in War* (New York, NY: W.W. Norton & Company, 1997), pp. 118–119.
5. Janina Bauman, *Winter in the Morning: A Young Girl's Life in the Warsaw Ghetto and Beyond 1939–1945* (New York, NY: The Free Press, 1986), p. 190.
6. National Institute of Mental Health, "Post-Traumatic Stress Disorder," Mental Health Education, https://www.nimh.nih.gov/health/topics/post-traumatic-stress-disorder-ptsd/index.shtml.
7. Bessel van der Kolk, "Posttraumatic Stress Disorder and Memory," *Psychiatric Times*, http://www.psychiatrictimes.com/ptsd/post traumatic-stress-disorder-and-memory.
8. Ezra BenGershôm, *David: Testimony of a Holocaust Survivor* (Oxford, England: Oswald Wolff Books, 1988), p. 278.

Glossary

alarmist A person who significantly exaggerates dangers, causing unnecessary worry.

anti-Semitism Fear and hatred of Jews.

Aryan One of the race categories popularized by racist biologists and anthropologists in the early twentieth century, primarily referring to white people of Nordic ancestry.

bunker An underground fortification or hiding place.

chancellor Head of state in a parliamentary government.

concentration camp A prison for civilians, political prisoners, and "enemies of the state," including Jews.

death camp A facility designed for mass murder, with gas chambers and crematory ovens.

dissident Someone who actively opposes the state.

Einsatzgruppen German killing squads that operated in the Soviet Union after the German invasion of June 1941.

emigrate To leave one country and settle in another.

final solution The term for the Nazi plan to solve what they called the "Jewish problem" or "Jewish question" by killing all the Jews in Europe.

gas chamber In Nazi Germany, a sealed room for killing groups of people; often disguised as a shower room.

Gentile A non-Jewish person.

Gestapo (Geheimestaatspolizei) Internal security police known for terrorist methods against persons suspected of treason or disloyalty to Nazi Germany.

ghetto A part of a city, usually viewed as undesirable, where minority groups are isolated.

liquidation Term Nazis used to mean "complete destruction." Sometimes the term was used to describe an action in which only some residents were either killed outright or transported to a death camp. In this case, the action was usually a step toward total destruction of the ghetto.

propaganda A one-sided communication, presenting a single point of view.

ration The amount of an item that was allowed. In the ghettos, food was rationed; each person was allowed only a certain, very small amount.

SS (Schutzstaffel) The paramilitary wing of the Nazi Party. Members of the SS served as camp guards and police.

visa Travel papers allowing a person to enter a country.

Further Reading

Books

Gruenbaum, Michael. *Somewhere There Is Still a Sun: A Memoir of the Holocaust*. New York, NY: Aladdin, 2015.

Lowry, Lois. *Number the Stars*. New York, NY: Houghton Mifflin Harcourt, 1989.

Miller, Sarah Lew, and Joyce B. Lazarus. *Hiding in Plain Sight: Eluding the Nazis in Occupied France*. Chicago, IL: Chicago Review Press, 2012.

Opdyke, Irene. *In My Hands: Memoirs of a Holocaust Rescuer*. New York, NY: Knopf, 1999.

Shackleton, Kath. *Survivors of the Holocaust*. London, UK: Hachette, 2016.

Skrypuch, Marsha Forchuk. *The War Below*. New York, NY: Scholastic, 2018.

Yolen, Jane. *Mapping the Bones*. New York, NY: Philomel Books, 2018.

Websites

BBC – The Holocaust Year by Year

http://www.bbc.co.uk/timelines/z86nfg8

An interactive timeline displaying the events of each year of the Holocaust.

History Channel Online

http://www.history.com/topics/world-war-ii/the-holocaust

The online branch of the History Channel offers videos and articles about the Holocaust more generally.

How Stuff Works: Stuff You Missed in History Class

https://www.missedinhistory.com/tags/world-war-ii.htm

A plethora of podcasts on all aspects of World War II.

The United States Holocaust Memorial Museum

www.ushmm.org/learn/students/the-holocaust-a-learning-site-for-students

The museum, located in Washington, DC, has a vast online archive of survivor interviews, informational articles, videos, and images.

Films

Defiance, dir. Edward Zwick, 2008.

"Escape from Auschwitz," April 29, 2008, *Secrets of the Dead: Unearthing History*, PBS, television program.

Index